The Christian's Duty and Safety in Evil Times
by Christopher Love
with chapters by C. Matthew McMahon

Copyright Information

The Christian's Duty and Safety in Evil Times, by Christopher Love, with chapters by C. Matthew McMahon
Edited by Therese B. McMahon

Copyright ©2019 by Puritan Publications and A Puritan's Mind™

Some language and grammar has been updated from the original manuscript. Any change in wording or punctuation has not changed the intent or meaning of the original author(s), and has been made to aid the modern reader.

Published by Puritan Publications
A Ministry of A Puritan's Mind™ in Crossville, TN.
www.apuritansmind.com
www.puritanpublications.com

All rights reserved. No part of this publication may be reproduced, stored in a retrieval system or transmitted in any form by any means, electronic, mechanical, photocopy, recording or otherwise, without the prior permission of the publisher, except as provided by USA copyright law.

This Print Edition, 2019
Electronic Edition, 2019
Manufactured in the United States of America

ISBN: 978-1-62663-331-5
eISBN: 978-1-62663-330-8

The Christian's Safety and Duty in Evil Times

Table of Contents

Love's Final Works 4

Meet Christopher Love 6

To the Christian Reader 13

SERMON 1: Christ's Prayer the Saint's Support 15

SERMON 2: A Divine Balance to Weigh All
Doctrines By 44

SERMON 3: A Christian's Great Enquiry 68

SERMON 4: A Description of True Blessedness 93

ANNEXED: The Saint's Rest, or Their Happy Sleep
in Death 108

Other Works by Christopher Love at Puritan
Publications 126

Love's Final Works
by C. Matthew McMahon, Ph.D., Th.D.

Much of what Christopher Love published in his day, or what his executors posthumously published after his death, has been reprinted today by Puritan Publications, and one other publisher from two decades ago (Soli Deo Gloria, now owned by Reformation Heritage Books). However, this volume is a spiritual treat, in that, it has never been published since the time Love's executors distributed it in 1653. To have this particular volume in print is exciting in that it houses the very last of Christopher Love's available works for publication. It is also bitter, in that, there are no more works by Mr. Love that we currently know about that could be published for us today.

It is true that the older publications of Love's reprinted works still need to be updated in more modern English, something I am doing methodically for Puritan Publications, but to bring forth a volume of his very last available unpublished works, is especially enlivening, and certainly helpful to the Christian's spiritual walk before Jesus Christ.

Annexed to Love's works in this volume in its original publication was a sermon given by Edmund Calamy, and it too is annexed to this volume, keeping in step with the original intention of Love's executors. It also has never been published, and this is the first time it has been in print since 1653.

My hope is that in all these works, you find the sweet marrow of Jesus Christ that Love so brilliantly pulls from the pages of Scripture for the good of your soul. He is, no doubt, one of the best and most simple preachers of Christ's Gospel to grace the church in the last 400 years. May you be blessed by your study along with him in these most important Scriptural texts and doctrines for improving your walk with God.

For *Christ's* glory,
C. Matthew McMahon, Ph.D., Th.D.
From my study, March, 2019.

Meet Christopher Love
by C. Matthew McMahon, Ph.D., Th.D.

Christopher Love (1618-1651), was a puritan minister, born at Cardiff, Glamorganshire, in 1618. He was the youngest son of Christopher Love, (having been given his father's name), and at fourteen years of age was converted under the preaching of William Erbury, an independent minister. His father disapproved of his religious impressions, and apprenticed him in London, where Erbury and Mrs. Love sent him to Oxford at their joint expense. He entered as a poor scholar of New Inn Hall under Dr. Rogers in June 1636, and graduated with a B.A. on May 2, 1639.

Mr. Wood says he was accustomed to ascend the pulpit of the church of St. Peter-in-the-Bayly at Oxford, and, "hold out prating," for more than an hour. On the other hand, his wife declares that he was often brought into the bishop's court, "for hearing of sermons."

Love was the first to refuse subscription to Laud's new canons of 1640, and although allowed to proceed to earn an M.A. On March 26, 1642, he was expelled from his congregation. In 1639 he proceeded to London on the invitation of Sheriff Warner to act as chaplain to his family. Here he met his future wife (Mary, daughter of Matthew Stone, formerly a merchant in London), who was the sheriff's ward. Subsequently Love received an invitation to become lecturer at St. Ann's, Aldersgate, but was for three years refused his pay by the bishop of London because he had not yet been ordained. Declining episcopal ordination, he went to Scotland to seek it at the hands of the presbytery; but was disappointed, as the Scottish Church had decreed to ordain only those who settled among them. He refused, "large offers," to stay in Scotland, and on his return to England, about 1641, preached at Newcastle, "by invitation," before the mayor and aldermen, when he expressed himself so freely against the errors of the *Book of Common Prayer*, he was committed to the common jail. He was subsequently removed to London on a document of *Habeas Corpus*,[1] was tried in the king's bench, and was acquitted.

About the outbreak of the civil war he preached as a lecturer at Tenterden, Kent, on the lawfulness of a defensive war, and was accused of treason, but he was acquitted and recovered his costs. Shortly afterwards he was made chaplain to Colonel Venn's regiment (see *State Papers*, Dom. 1642, p. 372), and when Venn was made governor of Windsor Castle, Love resided there as chaplain. Soon after the Presbyterian system was established in England during the Westminster

---

[1] A writ requiring a person under arrest to be brought before a judge or into court, especially to secure the person's release unless lawful grounds are shown for their detention. A *writ* is a form of written command in the name of a court or other legal authority to act, or abstain from acting, in some way.

Assembly, he was ordained in aldermanbury church by Mr. Horton and two others (the date by Thomas Brooks is January 23, 1644-1645 is impossible). While still residing at Windsor, he preached a provocative sermon in Uxbridge on January 31st, the day on which the commissioners were to treat the notion of peace between the king and parliament who had arrived in the town.[2] He asserted in his, "Vindication,"[3] that his preaching there was accidental and that none of the commissioners were present. On the complaint of the commissioners he was sent for by the commons and confined to the house during continuation of the negotiations. In 1645 he was nominated by ordinances of the lords and commons preacher at Newcastle[4] but does not appear to have gone there. On November 25th in the same year, he preached before the commons, and was not accorded the customary vote of thanks. Before 1647 he was settled as pastor at St. Ann's, Aldersgate, where he subsequently moved to St. Lawrence Jewry. As a zealous Presbyterian he soon made himself unbearable to the Independents.

    In 1651 he was accused of plotting against the Commonwealth. The affair is known as *Love's Plot*. He was charged with corresponding with Charles Stuart and with the prince's mother, (Henrietta Maria), between October 1649 and June 1651. It seems that Colonel Titus had been commissioned by certain

---

[2] *cf.* Lysons, Parishes in Middlesex are not described in the Environs of London, pp. 178-9.
[3] This is published as a separate volume by Puritan Publications called, *The Last Words and Letters of Christopher Love.*
[4] Barnes, *Memoirs*, p. 34.

Presbyterians to carry several letters to the queen-mother in France. The queen's replies were conveyed by Colonel Ashworth, and were read in Love's house in London. On December 18th, 1650 a pass was obtained for Love's wife to enable her to proceed to Amsterdam, without a doubt in connection with the same negotiations.

Love was ordered to be arrested on May 14th, 1651, and was committed as a prisoner to the Tower for high treason. He was tried before the high court of justice on June 20, 21, 25, and 27 and on July 5th, and was condemned to be executed on July 16th.[5] He was subsequently reprieved for a month, and then again for a week, but was finally executed on Tower Hill, Aug. 23rd, 1651, and privately buried at St. Lawrence Church.[6]

To the last of Love's petitions to the parliament, August 16th, he appends a "brief and full" narrative of the whole plot, in which he outlines all the charges made against him at the trial.[7]

Love had five children by his wife (who shortly after married Edward Bradshaw, mayor of Chester in 1653).

Love's works were:

1. "The debauched Cavalier, or the English Midianite," 1643.

---

[5] Thornwick, *Interregnum*, pp. 287.
[6] Robert Wilde wrote a poem on "The Tragedy of Mr. Christopher Love at Tower Hill," 1651, 4to.
[7] Both Kennett and Echard mention the story that a reprieve from Cromwell was intercepted and destroyed by furious royalists.

2. "England's Distemper, having Division and Error as its Cause, *etc.* Together with Vindication of the Author from...aspersions." London, 4to, 1645; having affixed the sermon preached at Uxbridge.

3. "Short and plaine Animadversions on some Passages in Mr. Dels' Sermon," 4to, London, 1646, 2nd edit. 1647.

4. "An Answer to an unlicensed Pamphlet," 4to, 1646, written in answer to the above.

5. "A modest and clear Vindication of the...ministers of London from the scandalous aspersions of John Price," *anon.*, London, 1649, 4to (ascribed to Love in *Illumination* to Sion College, 1649, anon.).

6. "A Cleare and necessary Vindication of the Principles and Practices of Mr. Christopher Love," *etc.*, 4to, London, 1651. His posthumously published petitions and narrative to the parliament, speech and prayer on the scaffold, and letters to his wife, were published in various unauthorized books in 1651. He also appears as editor, and may have been author, of "The Main Points of Church Government and Discipline," London, 1649, 12mo.

Love's executors, Edmund Calamy, Simeon Ashe, Jeremiah Whitaker, William Taylor, and Allan Geare, published after his death the following works:

1. "Grace, the Truth and Growth and Different Degrees Thereof (fifteen sermons)," 1652, 4to, and 1810.

2. "Heaven's Glory" (ten sermons), 1653, 4to, 1810; Dutch version, 1867 (Sneek, "De Neerligkheid das Hemels").*

3. "The Soul's Cordial, in two Treatises: (1) How to be eased of the Guilt of Sin, (2) Discovering Advantages by Christ's Ascension" (twenty-two sermons), 1653.
4. "A Treatise of Effectual Calling and Election," 1653.
5. "Scripture Rules to be observed in Buying and Selling," 1653.*
6. "A Christian's Duty and Safety in evil Times," 1653, to which is annexed the "Saints' Rest, or their happy Sleep in Death."
7. "The Hearer's Duty, and three other Sermons," 1653.*
8. "The Christian's Directory, tending to guide him," &c., 1653.*
9. "The true Doctrine of Mortification and Sincerity, in opposition to Hypocrisy," 1654.
10. "The Combat between the Flesh and Spirit" (twenty-seven sermons), 1654.
11. "The Sum or Substance of prelatical Divinity, or the Grounds of Religion in a catechistical Way," 1654.
12. "The dejected Soul's Cure, in divers Sermons," 1657.
13. "The Ministry of Angels to the Heirs of Salvation," 1657.
14. "Of God's Omnipresence," 1657.
15. "The Sinner's Legacy to Posterity," 1657.
16. "The Penitent Pardoned," 1657.
17. "A Discourse of Christ's Ascension and coming to Judgment."*
18. "The natural Man's Case stated, or an exact Map of the Worldly Man" (seventeen sermons), 1658.
19. "The History of the Holy Bible," 1783. His "Select Works," Glasgow, 2 vols. 8vo, appeared in 1805, and "Remains" (with life), London, 12mo, in 1807.
19. "Hell's Terror," (seven sermons), 1653.*

[Memoir in Quick's MSS., Dr. Williams's Library; biography, incomplete, by Love's wife, in Sloane MS. 3945; Foster's *Alumni Oxon.*; Wood's *Athenæ Oxon.* ed. Bliss; Cal. *State Papers.* Dom.; *State Trials*, vol. v.; Hist. MSS. Comm. 4th Rep. p. 365, 6th Rep. p. 435; Burton's *Diary.* ed. Rudd, ii. 88-9; Wilson's *Dissenting Churches of London*, i. 332, iii. 330; Notes and Queries, 1st ser. xii. 266, 2nd ser. iv. 173. 259, ix. 160, 291; Neal's *Puritans*, Brook's *Puritans*; Dugdale's *Treaty of Uxbridge*; Barnes's *Memoirs*, vol. 1. (Surtees Soc.); *Tracts* in Brit. Mus.]

Taken in part by the *Dictionary of National Biography*, 1885-1900, Volume 34, by William Arthur Shaw.

*These works have been republished by *Puritan Publications*.

To the Christian Reader

Although God has blessed Mr. Love with great abilities, yet, such as his humility, that he judged few or none of his sermons worthy for public view. This Mr. Love often said to his friends after he had received the sentence of death. Yet, it is admirable to consider what good entertainment all those works have found which have been published with his name. As by this providence, God put a great deal of honor on the name and memory of this good man. On this account, his dear widow and friends prevailed with, by importunity, to yield to printing more of his sermons, though they are not as full and exact as, without a doubt, they would have been if they had come from the author's pen.

The matter of these works are wholesome, seasonable, with a great savor of his gracious spirit who preached them. He manifests to the world the workings both of his heart and life, being zealously devoted to the service of Christ, and the Christian soul. This faithful minister of Christ, though he is dead, still speaks. And although he has finished his testimony on earth, yet he is still, by these works, serviceable in the land of the living.

Endeavor, in good earnest, to make a spiritual improvement of these topics, and other such helps to your soul, put by divine providence in your hand. And let the Lord be magnified in your conversation for all that soul-advantage which you may receive. Labor to be well rooted in the truths of the Gospel, bear up courageously against the evil of these deceiving times. And because so many shamefully disgrace their profession, by their carnal self-seeking, and apostasy, therefore, you should rather hold forth the power of godliness in the ways of self-denial, and faith, to the honor of Christ.

Your friends and servants,
Simeon Ashe
Edmund Calamy
Jeremiah Whitaker

SERMON 1:
Christ's Prayer the Saint's Support

"I pray not that thou shouldest take them out of the world, but that thou shouldest keep them from the evil," (John 17:15).

    This chapter in the book of John's Gospel contains in it the last and most solemn prayer, which we find on record, that Christ ever made in the world, with, and for his disciples. When he was to remove his person from them, even then he would leave a prayer behind him, that great legacy that he could give to them.

    The whole of chapter 17 from the beginning to the end is only made up of Christ's prayer to his Father. And in this solemn prayer, and the last prayer he made with his disciples, there are four things which we should observe.

1. The time when he made this prayer.
2. The gesture he used.
3. The manner how he prayed.
4. The matter for what he prayed.

    The time when he made this prayer is set down in two ways.

    1. It was immediately after he had preached a public sermon.[8] Observe then, that it is warrantable, and commendable, for minsters to pray after their public preaching. I tell you this because in this age there are a generation of men who judge otherwise. But it is set

---

[8] See the first part of the chapter.

down here in the practice of Jesus Christ himself, to do this. After he had preached, he lifted his eyes to heaven and prayed. And it is Martin Luther's note that, "a good prayer ought to follow a good sermon." And, by the way, take notice, that you who attend on the ministry of the Gospel must also go to God in prayer after you have heard his word. When we have finished preaching, then you must begin your praying. It is a good observation of holy Mr. Greenham, "I am persuaded that one great reason why there is so little good done by all our preaching, is, because though there is much preaching in the pulpit, yet, there is little or no praying in the closet."

The other circumstance of time when Christ made this solemn and affectionate prayer, is the day before he was going to die. For, as soon as he had finished this prayer, Judas came with a band of men to betray him (John 18:1-2). You should observe from Christ's example, that Christians should be most holy, and with ardent affections in their hearts when they are leaving this world behind in death. Jesus Christ prayed well at all times, but he prayed most affectionately a little time before he was to die. This passage of Scripture is very observable to this end, "And being in an agony he prayed more earnestly: and his sweat was as it were great drops of blood falling down to the ground," (Luke 22:44). When Jesus was in agony, and lay groveling on the ground, sweating great drops of blood, he prayed more earnestly,[9] or the Greek means he prayed more vehemently, drawing forth his affections to the uttermost. And the Apostle Paul speaking of this says, in

---

[9] ἐν ἀγωνίᾳ, ἐκτενέστερον προσηύχετο, (Luke 22:44).

Hebrews 5:7, "Who in the days of his flesh, when he had offered up prayers and supplications with strong crying and tears unto him that was able to save him from death, and was heard in that he feared."

Christ prayed with strong cries, alluding to that earnest prayer which he uttered in the garden, Luke 22:19, as appears by these words, "In that he feared," *viz.*, that bitter cup, those unspeakable pains, which he endured in his agony, when the whole power of darkness set on him. You see here that Jesus Christ prayed with a most fervent zeal and holy affection, just before he was to die. The Apostle is there treating of Christ's priesthood, and offering up himself as a sacrifice for sin.

Now, as it was with Jesus Christ, so should it be with you too. Before you come to die, you should then have the most holy, heavenly and ardent affections in your hearts. Let heaven at that time especially possess your souls, when your souls are going to possess heaven. O beloved, in this regard you should be like a swan which sings the sweetest songs before its death. Let your sweetest songs be like Simeon's.[10] When you come to die, say, "Lord, let thy servant depart in peace."

The second circumstance which is to be considered in the prayer of Christ, is the gesture he used while praying. "He lifted up his eyes to heaven and said, 'Father,'" *etc.* It is true, gestures are not simply necessary in any duty. It is not necessary to kneel in prayer, yet gestures may be helpful to us in prayer. Christ lifted up

---

[10] 'Lord, now lettest thou thy servant depart in peace, according to thy word,' (Luke 2:29).

his eyes to signify that his heart is where his eyes were. Beloved, when you lift up your eyes towards heaven in prayer, it should note that your heart is in heaven. I am sure, with Christ, it was this way, though with you it may be otherwise. It may be that your eye is towards heaven in prayer, when at the same time your heart is towards your work, towards some evil company, towards your whore, or wicked companions. Remember O man, to keep your heart as well as your eye towards heaven in prayer. Let your hearts and your eyes be both towards the same place. Christ lifted up his eyes to heaven in prayer, and his heart was there was well, and so it should be with you.

The third circumstance in Christ's prayer was the manner of praying. That is expressed in three ways in this chapter.

1. He aimed at God's glory as the chief end of all things which he prayed for. This should be a directory for your prayers as well. "Glorify thy Son, that thy Son also may glorify thee," (John 17:1). The end of Christ's prayer was to glorify his Father. So, the end of our prayers should be to glorify God.

Many men will cry, "Lord give me glory," when they do not with a longing heart say, "Lord, let me give glory to your name." Christ said, "Hallowed by thy name," expressing this respect to honor and glorify the name of God. That was the very first petition in Christ's prayer to show that to glorify God's name ought to be the first and chief thing in our prayers.

2. Christ prayed, "O my Father," to teach you that you must not only pray with an awful apprehension of God, but also with a faithful confidence in God. "But

without faith it is impossible to please him: for he that cometh to God must believe that he is, and that he is a rewarder of them that diligently seek him," (Heb. 11:6). You must never come to God to ask with doubt, but you must come with a faithful confidence, a fiducial confidence, as a child to a father.

3. Christ prays with great enlargement for the good of his disciples. I am not reading past verses 3-4 where Christ prayed for himself. The rest of his prayer was for his disciples, that God would keep them in unity and truth, and glorify them, and all other believers with himself in heaven. Here then, behold the wonderful affection that Jesus Christ bears to his church, and people, that when he was to die, he should pray more for saving their souls than for saving his own life. O! in this the superabundant love of Jesus Christ is manifested, who, when he was in expectation to die a painful, shameful, accursed death, undergoing the wrath of God do to us for our sins, yet, he would remember his elect servants. In their place he stood, and for their sins he died, with such an enlargement of his heart in prayer for them.

4. The fourth circumstance which is considerable in Christ's prayer is the matter itself; what he prayed. And that is laid down in two ways. 1. Negatively, who should not be the subject matter of his prayer, "I pray not for the world," (v. 9). This is a good argument against those who plead for universal redemption. If Jesus Christ would not spend his breath to pray for them, then surely he would not spend his precious blood to purchase heaven for them. Then it is laid down, 2. Affirmatively, whom he prayed for, "I pray

for them that thou hast given me, for they are thine." *You that are elected, you that are regenerated, I pray for you.* He makes many requests to his Father on behalf of his disciples that God would keep them, "that they might be one with him," (v. 11). That God would sanctify them (v. 17). That they might come to heaven and be with Christ, (v. 24). And, as in the text, "I pray not that thou shouldest take them out of the world, but that thou shouldest keep them from the evil."

The words, you see, are set down in two ways. 1. Negatively, what Christ did not pray for on behalf of his disciples, "I pray not that thou shouldest take them out of the world." 2. Affirmatively, what Jesus Christ did pray for, "I pray that thou shouldest keep them from the evil of the world." It may be demanded why Christ said these words, that he would not pray that his disciples might be taken out of the world.

Jesus Christ knew that his end was at hand, that his hour was coming, that he should depart out of the world. John 13:1, "Now before the feast of the Passover, when Jesus knew that his hour was come that he should depart out of this world unto his Father, having loved his own which were in the world, he loved them to the end." When the disciples heard this, they thought in this way with themselves, "Lord, if you will leave this world, what will become of us when you are gone? We shall be in the world as a ship without a pilot, or sheep without a shepherd. Therefore, they prayed that they might die with Christ, "Then said Thomas, which is called Didymus, unto his fellow disciples, Let us also go, that we may die with him," (John 11:16). And John 13:27 Peter said to him, ""Peter said unto him, Lord, why cannot I follow thee now? I will lay down my life for thy sake." The apostles were all on fire to die for Jesus Christ. Now, Christ seeing them so willing to die, so to check this impetuous motion, he tells them that he would not pray that they should now die, but he says, I will pray to my Father that when I am gone, and you remain behind in the world, that he would keep you from the evil of the world.

Now, if you should ask me what special reason there was why Jesus Christ would not pray that they might be taken out of the world, I will give you this answer.

Answer. 1. If the disciples had died when Jesus Christ died, then people would have thought that they had been sharers or co-partners with Christ in purchasing our salvation. Scripture says that Christ "did tread the wine-press of his Father's wrath alone, and that there was none with him," (Isa. 63:3). Christ will have the sole honor of our salvation. There were two common thieves, two unworthy people, that died with Christ, that the world might see that it was Christ's death alone that merited salvation for men.

2. A second reason is this, Christ did not pray that the disciples might be taken out of the world, because he had further work for them to do here in the world. As if he had said, "I have the Gospel for you to divulge and propagate, souls for you to convert, my elect to gather in. Therefore, I will not pray to the Father to take you out of the world, but to keep you from the evil of the world. Yet, I will not pray to keep you from afflictions and persecutions which for my name's sake you must expect to meet with in the world. Yet, I will

pray to keep you from the evil of sin, that you would not fall into sin through the allurements or frowns of the world, the malicious temptations of Satan, and the suggestions and inclinations of your own corrupt hearts when I am gone. I will pray that my Father would keep you from all evil of the times and place which you live."

3. The words in this way explained, I will draw out five conclusions from them.

First, from Christ's refusing to pray to his Father to take the disciples out of the world, they desire to die with Christ for fear of persecution. Here, observe a DOCTRINE: That it is not warrantable for any to wish for death because of persecutions and afflictions which they feel or fear. You find this was the fault of Jonah, in Jonah 4:3, "Now therefore O Lord I beseech thee, take away my life from me, for it is better for me to die than live." He said this in a pettish sickness, being displeased and angry that the Ninevites were spared, thinking that he should be accounted as a false prophet. Because of affliction or reproach in the world, to desire death is something that the Scripture does not warrant. There are three reasons for this.

1. Because your lives are great blessings, and you value them at too low of a rate when you rashly wish for death. It is true, there are some men that value their lives at too high a rate. They are such as will not lay down their lives for the sake of Jesus Christ, his truth and people, when they are called to this. There are others that value their lives at too low a cost, and they are those who wish to be taken out of the world because of troubles and afflictions that they meet with in the world.

Now, this is a sin. This is undervaluing your life, which is the greatest of all temporal blessings.

2. A second reason is this, because it is a more commendable thing to pray that God in due time would remove trouble from us, than to cry out, "Lord remove us from trouble." It is better to pray that God would sanctify our hearts patiently and thankfully to bear those crosses that he shall be pleased to exercise us with, rather than deliver us from trouble by taking us out of the world. God has ten thousand ways to free us from trouble, besides laying us in the grave. He can put an end to our troubles and yet lengthen out our lives.

3. There is more honor to be gained by a patient bearing of our burden then by being delivered from it. The soldier never grows famous for his valor until he comes to bear the brunt of battle in the field. And the Christian never shines in grace until he comes into the fire of afflictions; especially if he suffers in bearing witness to the truth of Christ. Therefore, we should be content, yes even rejoice, in our sufferings and not desire death to be rid of the troubles of this life.

Use. If this is true, that it is not warrantable for any man to desire death because of any affliction he fears or feels, then I draw a *use of reprehension* to many sorts of men in the world. I chiefly speak to you that are of a passionate and peevish spirit or have a forward and distempered soul. If God lays on you any affliction, if he mingles any crosses with your comforts, any gall and wormwood with your pleasant things, so that it may be that your estates are taken away, you are imprisoned, and your worldly comforts taken from you, O then in a peevish mood with Jeremiah, you curse the day of your birth. With Jonah you wish for the day of your death. Now, this is all sinful. It is true, good men have failed in this, as with Job, "O that I might have my request; and that God would grant me the thing that I long for! Even that it would please God to destroy me; that he would let loose his hand, and cut me off!" (Job 6:8-9). Here you see Job wishing for death, yes, even longing for it. He woos, as it were, destruction, and is an importunate and earnest suiter for the grave. All this was because God's afflicting hand was sorely on him. And we find him expressing the same distemper in the name of others. "Which long for death, but it cometh not; and dig for it more than for hid treasures," (Job 3:21). There is a sharpness and bitterness in bodily death, yet some are so afflicted in body and so oppressed in their spirit that they account the very bitterness of death to be sweetness. They see the gall and wormwood of affliction as sweet as honey, and as much longed for as the honey comb. And they do not only long for it, but they dig for it. And they do not do this in an ordinary way, but they dig as they would for treasure, yes, for hidden treasure, which shows the earnestness of this desire after death. This distemper also seized on the spirit of the prophet Elijah. "But he himself went a day's journey into the wilderness, and came and sat down under a juniper tree: and he requested for himself that he might die; and said, It is enough; now, O LORD, take away my life; for I am not better than my fathers," (1 Kings 19:4). The reason of this pettish desire in Elijah was because Jezebel, who had slain many of the Lord's prophets, threatened also to take away his life. It may be many of you to whom I speak have lost your estates, your work, now are in poverty, and lie under disgrace. You are apt and ready to go with God and pray that he takes you out of the world. But know, this is a very sinful frame of spirit, to long for death only to be freed from the trouble of this life, to desire to lie down in the bed of the grave only to ease our bodies, and rest our outward man. If we think life is not worth living or continuing in this world unless we enjoy our outward comforts, ease, plenty, prosperity, honor, wealth and friends, we by this very much undervalue the great blessing of life. This at best is an infirmity, and this idea Christ rebukes in his disciples.

Again, this is because Christ would not pray for his disciples to be taken out of the world when they desired death, fearing persecution.

A second doctrine to here to explain is this: that in some cases it is lawful for a man to desire to die.

First, when he does not desire it because of sufferings, but because of sins. When a man desires to shake off a body of flesh that he might be rid of, and freed from, this body of sin, this is commendable. This was Paul's prayer, "We are confident, I say, and willing rather to be absent from the body, and to be present with the Lord," (2 Cor. 5:8). To desire death is commendable, not because it kills your person and eases your pain, but because it kills your corruption and puts an end to your sinning. This is not like a little gate to lead you out into things temporary, but as a door out of the house to the street to let you onto eternal life. In this case, it is lawful.

2. It is lawful to desire death that you may by this have a fuller enjoyment of Jesus Christ. The apostle sets this down, "For I am in a strait betwixt two, having a desire to depart, and to be with Christ; which is far

better," (Phil. 1:23). For a man to desire to be dissolved that he may be without his crosses is a sin. But to desire to be dissolved that he may enjoy Jesus Christ is a grace. O! you that say, "I desire to die that I might have the enjoyment of God more perfectly and grace more completely," is a good desire. But to desire death because you shall have every tear and affliction wiped away is not. You should desire to have in death a white sheet to wipe away every sin, all temptations, all pollutions, which is a gracious desire. We are not to wish for death because our comforts are lessened, but that our communion with Christ might be completed. We should not see death as a door to let us out of troubles, but as a door to let us into heavenly mansions.

But passing by those things briefly, I proceed to another observation from these words, "I pray not that you might be taken out of the world." Why would not Christ make this prayer? The chief reason was because he had more work for his disciples to do in the world.

Observe, then, the third DOCTRINE: that it is not the desire of Jesus Christ that any of his servants should die, so long as he has any work for them to do in this world. Not only are your days numbered, not only the number of months with God, but likewise, the work that you will do which he has ordained for you to accomplish. God says to a minister, you shall preach so many sermons, convert so many souls, gather in so many of my elect. And when your work is done, your life will be over. You, godly Christian, until you have ended your work, you shall not end your days. This may be of great comfort to all that fear God. Do not fear death. It is not Christ's desire to take you out of the world until you have done all the work for which God has sent you into the world.

The use of this is threefold. First, for counsel, second for reproof, and the third for comfort.

1. Use of counsel to you all. 1) That you would desire to live not longer than that you might do the work for which God has you to do in the world. Do not desire to live that you may give into your lusts and do what you would like in your own eyes, but desire to live no longer than that you may serve God and do good to others.

2) It should teach you that you may be useful in the world, and so you should ask God, while you are useful, not to take you out of the world. I remember Martin Luther on this text has this note, "That it is the duty of a minister, more especially of them than any man in the world, to desire that his life may be prolonged, so that he may convert more souls to God." And it was the saying of an old minster when he was lying on his death bed, "Lord, if I may be useful to your people, let me live longer. I will not refuse more labor and more pains if you have more work for me to do." Any of you who may be useful in the world are bound to beg God that he would lengthen out your days, and that you may live to do more good in the place where God has set you.

3) Here, let me counsel you in this use. Though you suffer much evil from the world, yet if you can do much good in the world, let your doing good, rather, provoke you to desire life, then your suffering of evil to provoke you to desire death. We should rejoice in suffering much evil, provided that by suffering much evil we can do a great amount of good. When Cesar said, "I have lived long enough, where I respect nature or

honor," Tully answers, "Sire, though you have lived long enough for yourself, yet you have not lived long enough for your country." Are you a person that "doest good in thy generation," (Acts 13:36). Are you a useful person, though you might be old, and though infirmities of age might be upon you? Yet, do not let this make you weary of your life, though it may be that you think you have had a long enough time for yourself. Yet, consider, you have not lived long enough for others for the good of the church or commonwealth in which you live. Let this counsel sink into your hearts, seeing every mother's child is sent into the world to do something for God. O! labor, therefore, that when your days shall end, your conscience may tell you that you have done that work which God sent you into the world to do. It is the commendation of David in Acts 13:36, that "after he had served his own generation, by the will of God he fell asleep, and was gathered unto his fathers." He did his work and then he died.

O beloved, there is nothing in the world which will be a greater solace to your souls when you come to die (and we must all sooner or later drink of that cup) then this, that your conscience tells you, "I have served my God in my life, I have done my work, and the last work I have to do is to die." When your eyes are falling asleep, and your mouth is shut, and you cannot take any medicine to refresh your decayed spirits, then this will be a cordial for you. Conscience will tell you that you have done the work which God has given you to do. Do everything that God has sent you to do in the world. And now you have nothing to do but die and go to heaven. It is an observable expression, "Thou shalt come to thy grave in a full age, like as a shock of corn cometh in in his season," (Job 5:26). You know, that if a man should reap a stock of corn when it is green, and newly growing an ear, that corn will be of no use for making bread. But if he cuts down a shuck of corn when it is ripe, it is useful to make bread. Death cuts off many men that are green corn, unfit, unprepared for death, unripe for heaven, unripe for glory. This is when they are like grass on the house top, that withers before it is cut down (Psalm 127:6). They are like seed which fell on stony or thorny ground which never came up to perfection. But now, God says to the good man, when you have done your Master's work, then shall you go to your Master's mansion. You shall come to the grave like a shuck of corn in its due season. O! what comfort and solace of heart should this be to you who have done the world for which God sent you into the world.

  2. The use of reproof. Is it true that Christ does not desire that any of his servants should die until they have done the work for which God sent them into the world? Then this may reprove the wicked of the world who come to die before they begin to do that work for which they came into the world. Are there not many that have lived to have gray hair, and are hastening to the grave, those who never put their hands to any work which God sent them into the world to do? Beloved, I would leave you one sad text of Scripture, and it is worthy to be engraved in gold. "There shall be no more thence an infant of days, nor an old man that hath not filled his days: for the child shall die an hundred years old; but the sinner being an hundred years old shall be accursed," (Isa. 65:20). This is the most dismal text that

I know of in the Old Testament to wicked men. Yet, it is comfortable to the godly. It is a promise of the conversion and bringing in of the Gentiles. I will explain its sense in this way, that is, there are people that have lived many days, and many years, and yet have no more knowledge of God, have done no more service to God than an infant. There were many like this in the time of the prophets. These people were old, yet infants in their understanding and knowledge. "nor shall there be an old man, that hath not filled his days." This means that the old man that does not do anything in grace, that does not serve and glorify God, that does not fulfill the duty of every day, that fills his days with sin, and not with righteousness, this is the man that has not filled up his days rightly. There are many such old men in the world, whose wrinkled faces and gray hairs declare them to be eighty years old, yet in regard of grace and knowledge, they have not come to be 14 years of age. Now how may this justly be for rebuke to any of you who are infants in this, who have done God no more service, and are no more acquainted with God than children. You have lived many days, but they have been empty days. Your hearts are full of sin, and it is no wonder then, that they are so empty of grace. Is there not many men and women who may with shame and sorrow in this way reflect on themselves before God in this way:

"Have I not lived 40, 60 maybe 80 years, yet, Lord, you know, my days are empty days. I have not done any good all my lifetime." In Scripture, when good men die, they are said to die in a good old age. But an old drunkard, and old adulterer, or an old swearer dying in old age is a bad old age, not a good old age. When you come to die, then conscience will reflect on you and say, "I am an old man, but I have not done the world which God sent me in the world to do." I read of an old disciple who was 90 years old, and was asked a question. They asked him, "How old are you?" He answered, "45 years of age." They said, "Your gray hairs show you to be much more than that." He said, "If you are reckoning a total number of years then yes, I am 90 years old. But if I compute how long I have devoted life to God, then I am but 45; for the other half of my time I lived as a dead man." O! how many people are there in the world that live most of their life as a dead man? There is a passage in Eccl. 7:17, "Be not over much wicked, neither be thou foolish: why shouldest thou die before thy time?" Some interpreters take it this way, "A man walking in drunkenness, excess and such, as it were, shortens his days." Others think, "that he which in this way lives is dead while he lives, before his time of death, and when death comes, he is twice dead." Indeed, a man cannot die before God's time. "Seeing his days are determined, the number of his months are with thee, thou hast appointed his bounds that he cannot pass," (Job 14:5). It is true that you cannot die before your time. But most people come to die before they are prepared to die and fitted to die. If you die in this way before you have done your work which God has given men to do, then you are the man that dies before your time. That is the way I take those words in the text. O! think about it, though you cannot die before God's time, you may die before your time, before you are fitted for death, before you have done things the world God gave you to do in this life. If Jesus Christ prayed that his disciples might not die before they had done their work, then what blame do they have, (even if they should live until doom's day)? Is this an excuse for you that God should not be given any more service than he now has from you, and no more? Are you one in whom he should see as much sin then as he does now instead of working to righteousness?

3. The next use is a use of comfort. If it is that Jesus Christ does not desire that his people should be taken out of the world until they have done all their work, then all you that are God's people should know that as long as God continues to let you live here in this world, he has work for you to do. Suppose you are thrown into prison. Consider that as part of your work here that you must do before Jesus Christ. If you are a minister of the Gospel and are under poverty, reproach, or cruel persecution for righteousness sake, consider that this is part of the service that you are to do for God. Christ will not take you away when you have only done half your work. He will take you when you have finished your work, then you will go to receive your wages. I remember the saying of Rev. Robert Bolton, when he was on his death bed, "O Lord, this is my comfort, that though I have ended my days, yet I have done my work before I die." This is a comfort to a godly heart. But for the wicked this is dreadful. When you have ended your days, and have not begun your work, and have not begun to serve God, this will be a great gouging of your conscience to you another day. This will be a worm that will gnaw on you in hell to all eternity, to remember that God set you out in your work to do this in the world while you lived here, and promised you both the time and the means to finish it. But you trifled away your time

and sinned away many heavenly opportunities of grace and mercy, played all day along, when you had so much work to do. When your days were at an end, you have not even begun to work. As it was with Charles, the king of Sicily, who cried out with a consternation of heart, "I have not begun to live, and yet I am going to die." O! do not let this guilt lie on your conscience. Do not let this be the worm to gnaw you in hell, to remember that you lived long in the world and yet did not do the work for which God sent you into the world.

Now, I proceed to the fourth observation out of these words, "I pray not that you might be taken out of the world." Observe here the fourth DOCTRINE: that no man dies but that God takes him away. If our lives were in our own hands, we would live too long. If our lives were in our enemy's hands, we would not live a day longer. But our lives are in God's hands, and therefore we cannot die, but God must take away our lives. And this may show a Christian his shelter under divine protection. A wicked man cannot thrust you out of the world before your time. God must take you out of the world. It may be, enemies may bear a grudge against you, and those who hate you may wish you a thousand deaths. Yet, here is your comfort, you cannot die before God takes you out of the world. In Scripture, when men die, they are said to be "gathered to their fathers." You will live until God shall think it right to gather you to himself, having made you fit for glory. And in this way I have opened the first branch of the text, "I pray not that thou shouldest take them out of the world."

Now I come to show what it is that Christ prays for on behalf of his disciples. "But I pray that thou wouldest keep them from evil." He means here, I do not pray that you would take them out of the world, but that you would keep them from falling into sin, from falling finally away from you. Here is my prayer, that you would keep them from the evil of the world. Observe here the fifth DOCTRINE: that it may be a great comfort to the people of God that they have the prayers of Jesus Christ to keep them from evil while they live in this world. Though Jesus Christ does not pray for you that you should be taken out of the world, yet he does pray for you that you may not sin in the manner and at that rate as the world sins. You may not yield to the devil's temptations in such a way as the world does. This is the great prayer of Jesus Christ.

Now, there are two questions that I shall answer.

It is true, the perplexed heart says, I do believe that Jesus Christ did pray for his eleven apostles, that God would keep them from the devil's temptations and from sin in the world. But does Christ pray for me that have lived so many years since that time?

Answer. Jesus Christ knew that this objection would arise in the hearts of his people in the following ages. Therefore, Christ himself resolves this objection in John 17:20, "Neither pray I for thee alone, but for them also which shall believe on me through their word." Christ does not say, I pray for all. If he did, he would contradict what he said formally in the ninth verse where he says, "I pray not for the world, but for them that thou hast given me, for they are thine." 1. All that God the Father has given to Christ, all believers are within that compass of Christ's prayer, but not all those in the world. 2. Again, he does not say, I pray for all that do believe, for then it might have been confirmed to the believers of that time in which Christ lived on earth. But I pray for them that shall believe, so that the prayer of Jesus Christ for keeping them from the evil of the world extends to all believers until the world ends. 3. Again, he does not say, I pray for all Jews that shall believe, but he says, for all in general, whether Jew or Gentile, Barbarian of Scythian, bond or free, what or whomever they are. I pray for all that shall believe. This prayer of Christ is not impaled or confined to only the apostles, but the efficacy and benefit of this is transferred to all believers to the world's end. Jerome says about this, which is a good observation, "Christ does not say, I pray for all that have shed their blood for me, then only martyrs should have the benefit of Christ. Neither does Christ say, I pray for all that convert souls to me, then only preachers should have benefits by Christ. But I pray for you that do and shall believe in me." In this way, *every Christian* has a share and benefit, in the prayer of Christ.

A second question is this: it is indeed true, (some may say) that when Christ was on the earth, his prayer then was of use, but can I imagine to have fruit and benefit by that prayer which Christ made then on earth?

Answer. I answer this, that the efficacy of Christ's prayer continued after Christ's time, as may appear by this illustration. If Stephen's prayer became efficacious for Saul's conversion, after Stephen was by his consent stoned to death, (for when Stephen was dying, he prayed that God would forgive them) then shall not the prayer of Christ himself become efficacious after his death?"

Again, Christ himself says, that his prayer on earth should be for all those that should believe afterwards, so that, this very prayer of Christ to God the Father, to keep them from evil, is as efficacious in this generation, and will be to the world's end, as it was at the very hour it was made.

Secondly, suppose it was true, that the prayer of Christ was not efficacious now, yet there is no doubt to be made, but that Christ's intercession now in heaven is efficacious, for he sits at God's right hand making intercession. "Who is he that condemneth? It is Christ that died, yea rather, that is risen again, who is even at the right hand of God, who also maketh intercession for us," (Rom. 8:34). And, "For Christ is not entered into the holy places made with hands, which are the figures of the true; but into heaven itself, now to appear in the presence of God for us," (Heb. 9:24). So that here is your comfort, that though it should be true that the efficacy of this prayer did not continue to this generation, yet it is undoubtedly true that the efficacy of Christ's intercession now in heaven continues for you to the world's end. Christ lives forever to make intercession for you.

Now I shall handle six practical inferences which this doctrine affords to us.

Is it so that Jesus Christ prays for all his people, *viz.*, disciples then, and believers now, that they should be kept from evil while they live in this world? I infer the following then.

1. That, therefore, we ourselves should entreat God to keep us from evil. Jesus Christ's prayer for us should not exclude our own praying for ourselves.

Christ never intended to pray to his Father to keep us from sin, that we should then be careless, and never pray to keep ourselves from it. Although Christ prays to keep us from evil, yet we must also pray this too. He teaches us in Matthew 6:13, "And lead us not into temptation, but deliver us from evil." This is the same point even in this prayer. It is an observation of Gerard in his *Harmony*, where he says, "The prayers of Jesus Christ were not only meritorious, but they were also exemplary, to teach us what and how we should pray." Did Christ pray that I might be kept from sin, from the evil of the time and place in which I live. Should not this then teach me to pray that God would keep me from the temptations and snares that I may meet with in the world, and that lie in my way to heaven? Christ's prayer must not exclude your prayers. It is said in Luke 22:40, "And when he was at the place, he said unto them, pray that ye enter not into temptation." It was not for them to say, Christ prayed for us, therefore what need do we have to pray for ourselves? No, Christ says, though I pray for you, yet pray for yourselves also, that you do not enter into temptation. This is my first inference, that Christ's prayers must not exclude our prayers.

2. Second inference. If this is a truth, that Christ prays to keep you from evil in the world, then, let this be a comfort to your hearts. It was to Peter's, "And the Lord said, Simon, Simon, behold, Satan hath desired to have you, that he may sift you as wheat, but I have prayed for thee, that thy faith fail not: and when thou art converted, strengthen thy brethren." (Luke 22:31-32). It may be that you have not minded this passage, but there is a great deal of comfort in it. It is said that Satan desired to

winnow Peter, to tempt Peter, but at that time the Lord Jesus was actually praying for Peter. Before the devil tempts you to embrace a temptation, Christ actually prays for you, that you may not be overcome with temptation. When the devil purposes to tempt you, Christ prays to prevent the peril. Christ does not only pray in the time of your temptation when the devil makes a strong incursion and violent invasion on your soul. But before the devil even sets on you, Christ is praying for you, "Satan has desired to winnow you, but I have prayed for you." O! then, think in your heart, I see the devil is very busy with my poor soul, soliciting and provoking me to work wickedness. But now reflect and remember that Christ is in heaven praying for you. As the devil tempts me to yield, Christ prays that I may not yield through the strength which he has given me. Now this may be a ground for wonderful comfort, to remember that Christ prays for you, that you may not be overcome with the evils of the world.

 3. The third inference is, that this should be a check to control your lust. In other words, to remember that Christ prays for you. Whenever the devil solicits you to any sin, think in this way to yourself: I see now the devil is very busy with me, to tempt me to this way of wickedness. But shall I dare to cross my own prayers? No. Shall I dare cross the prayer of Jesus Christ? For as Christ prayed on earth, so he now is praying in heaven for me that I may not yield to this temptation. Shall I make void the prayer of my Lord and Savior Jesus Christ? When Christ prays to his Father to give me strength to resist temptation, shall I carelessly run myself into temptation?

4. A fourth inference is this, *viz.*, that Christ's praying to his Father to keep you from evil must not lessen your care to keep yourselves from evil. It is a wretched use which is made of the indulgence of God the Father, and the intercession of Jesus Christ, that when these shall make you presumptuously bold and securely careless in how you live. Christ (I am sure) bids you to pray, that you *enter not into temptation.* You and I must so watch against temptation, as if I had no one to watch the devil but myself, and so pray against temptation as if I had no one to pray against it but myself. Yet, when I have prayed and watched, and been kept from the devil's temptation, I must ascribe all to the mercy of God and prayer of Christ, and nothing to myself.

5. The fifth inference is this, does Christ pray that you might be kept from evil? Then learn here that there is a proneness in our nature to be defiled with the evil of the times and places in which we live. Christ would never have prayed to his Father for us, unless there had been a strong inclination in our nature, and minds, to be defiled with the evils of the world.

6. The sixth inference is this, if Jesus Christ prays to his Father to keep us from the evils of the world, then here learn, that every man by nature is unable to keep himself from the evil of the world. The devil is "a strong man armed," (Luke 11:21), and you are an unarmed poor creature. He is stronger than you, and you can with as much ease subdue and overcome an army of a hundred thousand men, as kill one lust by your own power. It is a good note that Augustine makes on these words, "without me ye can do nothing." He says, "Christ does

not say, without me you can do little, but without me you can do nothing. The least work, if it is a work of grace, cannot be done without Jesus Christ." O! then, see the feebleness and frailty of your nature, you can do nothing without Christ, you cannot make a little prayer, you cannot subdue the least corruption without Jesus Christ. O! this should make us see our inability that Christ is driven to pray to his Father for us, to keep us, because we cannot keep ourselves. The mother holds the child, and the child holds the mother, but the strength lies not in the child, but in the mother. You fly to Christ, and lay hold on Christ, and that is well done. But the strength does not lie there. Christ goes to his Father, and prays to his Father, and says, *Father keep such a poor soul that when he is tempted he may not yield and he may not fall.* O! your strength lies in this, that Christ goes to his Father and prays that you will not yield to such a temptation of the devil, or at least that you may not be finally overcome. As it was with Peter, though he was foiled and sinned, yet his faith did not fail.

In further application of the doctrine, consider that if Jesus Christ prays to his Father to keep you from evil, O! then, I entreat you all to carry yourselves in this way in the world, that you labor to accomplish the prayer of Jesus Christ. If you shall ask me, how may I do that? I answer in this way.

I give you five directions to accomplish the prayer of Christ.

First, when you are tempted to any sin, avoid all disputing with the devil, all reasoning with flesh and blood about the sweetness and profitableness of such a sin. Disputing will get you nowhere. Therefore, when the devil comes to tempt you to sin, tell him that you are not at leisure to hear him. You have better work to do, and a better rule to walk by. You have the Spirit's motion to hear, and not his injections to dally with.

Secondly, avoid all occasions to sin. If you are inclined to drunkenness, do not go into bad company. Avoid the bar. If you are inclined to lust, avoid the company of lewd women, and that is the way, through the grace of God, to keep away from evil. It is said of the young wanton in Proverbs 7:8, that when he desired to be unclean, "He walked in the streets where the harlot dwelt." First, he went to the corner of the street, then to the harlot's door, and then the devil got power over him, to lead him into the house. When you run boldly and adventurously to the brink of sin, and lead yourself into temptation, do not wonder why you have been overcome. By an inconsiderate dallying with the occasions of sin, you tempt the devil to tempt you. And when once the devil feels your pulse, he will provide a suitable temptation for you. Whereas, if you didn't dread the fire, you would not be burned. If you are careful to avoid the beginnings of sin, and occasions to sin, that would be a means to keep you from evil.

3. Consider the all-seeking eye of God is on you. Wherever you are, and whatever you are doing, even when you are contriving the most secret way of sin, he sees you. This consideration had a powerful effect on Job. "I made a covenant with mine eyes, why then should I think on a maid? ...doth not he see my ways and count all my steps?" (Job 31:1, 4). God sees my heart, and sees my ways, therefore, I do not dare to think, much less act, anything that is wicked. Consider that the all-seeing eye

of God is on you, and this is a preservative to secure you from sin, yes, this is the way that God has sanctified you to keep you from the evil of the world. If you do evil with the world, you shall be punished with the world. If you run with the stream, you will be drowned in the stream. If you sin with the wicked, you shall be damned with the wicked.

4. To keep you from the evil of the times, consider that it is less of a danger to be under the suffering of the evil of the times, than it is to be under the sinning evil of the times. If you will not run with the stream, and walk wickedly, as the rest of the world does, then it may be you may be exposed to the suffering evil of the times. But it is better for you to lie in a prison than to sin by any conniving at, abetting of, or compliance with the unparalleled wickedness that have been of late done among us, and are yet doing. O! you had a thousand times better endure to the utmost extremity, all the suffering evil that the times may bring on you then to have any hand in the sins of the times, which are astonishing and amazing.

5. When you are tempted to any sin, make your recourse to Jesus Christ, flee to him for refuge because you stand by Christ's strength and not by your own strength. If you reflect on all this to yourself, consider thinking in this way: alas, I have prayed, I have shed many tears, I have heard many sermons, and yet I cannot kill my lusts nor subdue my corruptions. But yet there is one means left for me to use, and that is to flee to Jesus Christ, and to call to mind his mediation for me, his praying for me, and on my behalf. Christ does not only pray in heaven to save your soul, but he also prays to

sanctify your affections, and to enable you to resist temptations. Not only to save your soul, but for all other things that are subservient to your salvation. O! it is a great comfort that you have one more string in your bow that the world cannot break. Though all your strength fails, your heart fails, and all fail, yet you have the prayers of Jesus Christ which never fail. O! this prayer of Christ should be a great means to uphold you and keep your soul, "I pray not that thou shouldest take them out of the world, but that you should keep them from the evil."

SERMON 2:
A Divine Balance to Weigh All Doctrines By

1 Thessalonians 5:21, "Prove all things; hold fast that which is good."

In the latter part of this chapter the Apostle lays down many practical conclusions to be observed and performed by us in our Christian course and conversation. He begins in the 14th verse and ends at the 22nd verse. And in this you have 12 or 13 excellent conclusions which are as it were an epitome of our whole duty both towards God and man. *Warn them that are unruly. Comfort the feeble-minded. Support the weak. Be patient towards all men. Render not evil for good unto any man. Ever follow that which is good both amongst yourselves and all men. Rejoice Evermore. Pray without ceasing. In everything give thanks. Quench not the spirit. Despise not prophesyings. Prove all things hold fast that which is good. Abstain from all appearance of evil.* Now the words of the text are almost the last but they are not counted as the least duty here prescribed.

Interpreters take pains to give, not only the sense, but the dependence of these words, on the former. I shall not trouble you with the connection, but only make you aware of that which goes immediately before the text, in other words, *despise not prophesyings.* Prophesying in this place is not taken for that great, and extraordinary gift which the prophets had, both of the Old Testament and also in the New Testament by which they were able by God to foretell things to come by immediate revelation and to interpret the scripture with an unerring spirit. Now this extraordinary kind of prophesying is ceased, the Lord having fully revealed in the scriptures whatsoever is necessary to be known touching on the state of his church even to the end of the world. So that by prophesying here is meant only preaching. 1 Corinthians 14:31, "You may all prophesy one by one that all may learn and all may be comforted." That is, preach one by one, for it would make everything confusing in the congregation for too many to speak at once. It is observable to whom the Apostle gave this injunction, not to the wicked of the world, but to the Thessalonians. These were not Christian babes in Christ, as the Philippians were. They were strong Christians, grown Christians who had gained a great measure of faith, patience and holiness as 1 Thessalonians 1:7, "you were examples to all that believe in Macedonia and in Acadia." They were Christians of the upper form, famous for faith and godliness, exemplary to neighbor churches, yet the Apostle bids them to not despise prophesying. Not to despise the preaching of the word of God. There are and in our days many vein and ignorant people, who out of fantastical conceit of their own perfection and knowledge, and high achievement of glory, think that they are above all of God's ordinances. They think that they are above prayer, hearing the word, or receiving the sacrament. They live all together in excess. You shall never see them below the third heaven; their common just course is of an *expressed* ravishing communion with the Lord Jesus Christ not an actual one. And on this they condemn all the ordinances of the Gospel, they think of them as beggarly rudiments, as children's food. But let such consider, that if any church or people in the world might have pleaded that they were above God's ordinances, the Thessalonians might have done it who were in every way gracious, even beyond comparison. Yet the Apostle presses on them the necessity of attending on the gospel ministry. Here is an observation: that men may have obtained the highest perfection of grace and knowledge, that is possible for men in this life to obtain, and they are not, even at that stage of their sanctification, to despise or neglect the ordinances of Jesus Christ. Not only does a child need daily food, but the strongest man in the world will faint and die without it. I have wondered to think how the devil could ever get his deceit into the hearts of men, to make them think that they are above all God's ordinances. The Scriptures speak so expressly against this opinion. "Wherefore tongues are for a sign, not to them that believe, but to them that believe not: but prophesying serveth not for them that believe not, but for them which believe," (1 Cor. 14:22). Here you see that the Apostle clearly asserts that believers, even strong believers, are not to despise prophesying. And David, a great prophet and man after God's own heart, who was rich in gifts and grace, still longs "after God's presence in the tabernacle," (Psalm 84:2). The presence of God was his earnest desire, his chief comfort that he accounted it the greatest happiness that he could attain to in this world. He wanted to be near the ark of God, where it was, the place of God's residence among men in those days, to behold the face of God in his sanctuary, to enjoy the public ordinances of God. And the Apostle says, "But strong meat belongeth to them that are of full age, even those who by reason of use have their senses exercised to discern both good and evil," (Heb. 5:14). *Those who are of full age*, i.e. in comparison to those he before compared to babes. *By reason of use, i.e.* by hearing, reading and meditating on the word of God. *Have their senses, i.e.* their understanding, judgment and memory. *To discern both good and evil, i.e.* to choose that which is good, and to refuse that which is evil. Now the Apostle expressly says in Ephesians 4:11-13, "And he gave some, apostles; and some, prophets; and some, evangelists; and some, pastors and teachers; For the perfecting of the saints, for the work of the ministry, for the edifying of the body of Christ: Till we all come in the unity of the faith, and of the knowledge of the Son of God, unto a perfect man, unto the measure of the stature of the fulness of Christ." The use of the ministry is perpetual. It is to continue so long as the sun and moon endure, until all the elect of God are brought in. It is to continue until we come to be perfect men, which shall be in the world to come. We must live under the means of grace until we come to glory.

And the reasons for this are the following. 1. Because our sanctification in this life is not perfect. The Scripture last quoted intimates this to us. There is the old man and the new man, flesh and spirit in the best of saints even though sin has received its deadly wound and it shall never reign over them. Yet, such remaining sin may tyrannize us, and we shall never be perfectly freed from its rebellion until we come to heaven.

The heart is exceedingly deceitful, "deceitful above all things," (Jer. 17:9). The heart of man is the greatest cheater in the world. There is no deceiver that is so wicked, so unsearchably wicked, beyond all expression, *who can know it?* Wickedness lies hidden in its secret corners. There is not a man, no not the most knowledgeable and most innocent man, who "knoweth how often he offendeth," (Psalm 19:12). Solomon says here in Proverbs 28:26, "He that trusteth in his own heart is a fool." Now the preaching of the word is an effectual means for the removing of corruption, and discerning the secret turnings and wandering of the heart. Hebrews 4:12, "For the word of God is quick, and powerful, and sharper than any two edged sword, piercing even to the dividing asunder of soul and spirit, and of the joints and marrow, and is a discerner of the thoughts and intents of the heart." I thought it would be good to show you this, that while you live in the world, you are to wait on the ministry of the word, and not to despise preaching.

Now after the Apostle's injunction, my text comes fitly in this place. Many will despise the minister's doctrine before they try it. Therefore, the apostle subjoins "Despise not prophesying" with "prove all things." Try, try, and if there is any error in what you hear, then despise it. Do not despise preaching, only this is the work you are to do, "Try all things, and hold fast that which is good."

In the first place, I want to give you the meaning of the Greek words here, "prove," which is the word δοκιμάζετε (1 Thess. 5:21), and is borrowed from the gold smiths. When they would try their metal to find out if it was good or not, they would bring it to the magnetic touchstone. So, the word itself signifies to *try*, or to know by experience. So, you are to try all the doctrines you hear by the touchstone of the word. That is the standard, to try them. Try or prove all things, and by all things here is meant all doctrines preached, all prophesyings or preaching you hear. It is to be noted and observed that when the Apostle Paul spoke these words, the Gospels were not written yet, nor commended to the public care of the church of God. It is thought that this epistle was written thirty years or more before the Gospels. Now in that, the Apostle commands them to try the doctrines preached. He in this refers them to the Scriptures of the Old Testament. Then the phrase follows, *hold that which is good.* There is a twofold *holding fast.* 1. A holding fast in judgment the truths of the Gospel, that you do not run into error. And, 2. A holding fast in practice the power of the Gospel, that you do not run into sin.

1. Hold fast in judgment the truths of the Gospel that you do not run into error. This is laid down in 2 Peter 3:17, "Ye therefore, beloved, seeing ye know these things before, beware lest ye also, being led away with the error of the wicked, fall from your own stedfastness." What he means in this is judgment. There must be a foreknowledge of the truths of the Gospel before you can attain to be steadfast in grace. And besides knowledge, there is required vigilance and carefulness if we would hold fast the truths of the Gospel. In this way, you are to retain in judgment the doctrines of the Gospel, that you do not run into erroneous principles. It is childish, Paul says, "That we henceforth be no more children, tossed to and fro, and carried about with every wind of doctrine, by the sleight of men, and cunning craftiness, whereby

they lie in wait to deceive;" (Eph. 4:14). This is to be over credulous, easy of belief, fickle, and answering in the way a child does.

2. It implies holding fast in practice, that you do not run into sin so that you hold on your course of holiness, being settled and unaltered. And this is laid out when Paul says, "That ye may be blameless and harmless, the sons of God, without rebuke, in the midst of a crooked and perverse nation, among whom ye shine as lights in the world; Holding forth the word of life; that I may rejoice in the day of Christ, that I have not run in vain, neither laboured in vain," (Phil. 2:15-16). What he means here is in a blameless, holy and humble conversation. A man then holds fast when he frames his life according to the direction of the word of God. For knowledge is empty and vain, and does not profit, if it is not reduced to practice. And practice in our Christian course is difficult up the hill. It requires great heed and watchfulness. So, we must be solicitously careful to hold out in our practice what we are convinced in our judgment is the truth and the will of God revealed in the word. So, the sense of the words here are this, try all the doctrines of that minister under which you live by the word of God, whether they are true or false, sound or corrupt. What you find to be the truth, and conforms to the word of God, embrace it, hold it fast in your just judgment, that you do not run into any contrary opinions. In your practice, do not run into any vicious courses in your lives and conversation. And what you find to be false and sinful, reject it. And so, you have a brief paraphrase and explanation of the words. From the

first part of the words, prove all things, I will draw out a number of observations and doctrines.

DOCTRINE: that it is the duty of all hearers of the word to try and prove all those doctrines which they hear. It is the injunction that the Apostle John gives in his first epistle, "Beloved, believe not every spirit, but try the spirits whether they are of God: because many false prophets are gone out into the world," (1 John 4:1). That is, try the doctrines that such men preach, who pretend that they have the Spirit, and preach by the Spirit, whether they are preaching true or false. Erroneous teachers will boast of the Spirit, and so, we must try what spirit their doctrine comes from. We must not, as with Solomon's fool, give credence to everything that is published under the glorious name of truth. But we must consider that the church of God always has been pestered with false teachers. In Jeremiah's time there were such as published the visions of their own mind for sound doctrine. And the Apostle Paul often complains of false teachers that *transformed themselves into angels of light*. It is the devil's policy to many times transform himself into an angel of light. And because his commodities will not sell in his own making, he labors to bring them into God's market (for such is the preaching of the word) thinking that none will suspect them there. Have we not then great reason to try all doctrines that we hear?

In handling this doctrine, I will first give some cautions. Secondly, I will give some reasons of it. Thirdly, I will lay down some directions about trying what you hear.

The first caution is this, when the apostle bids you "prove all things" he does not intend by this that people should have liberty to hear anyone and so try all preachers. As Calvin pointed out on this passage, for, by this means a man may sooner suck in an error than embrace the truth. No, the Scripture is expressly against it. If you can hear a man that preaches the truth, you are not to follow such as are known to divulge errors. "For the time will come when they will not endure sound doctrine; but after their own lusts shall they heap to themselves teachers, having itching ears; And they shall turn away their ears from the truth, and shall be turned unto fables," (2 Tim. 4:3). And John says, "If there come any unto you, and bring not this doctrine, receive him not into your house, neither bid him God speed: 11 For he that biddeth him God speed is partaker of his evil deeds." (2 John 1:10). And also, "Then if any man shall say unto you, Lo, here is Christ, or there; believe it not. For there shall arise false Christs, and false prophets, and shall shew great signs and wonders; insomuch that, if it were possible, they shall deceive the very elect. Behold, I have told you before. Wherefore if they shall say unto you, Behold, he is in the desert; go not forth: behold, he is in the secret chambers; believe it not," (Matt. 24:23). False prophets shall arise, and what will they say? Here and there is Christ. Not as if Christ was there personally, but doctrinally. Some shall say he is in the desert, for these false teachers used to draw people out into desert places where they might more securely publish their errors and heresies. Whereas, truth seeks no corners to hide. But, *go not out after them*, Christ says, *If they shall say he is in a secret chamber, do not believe them.* Things that are honest always rejoice in being made public, but viciousness wants to be concealed. Therefore, it is that they seek out secret chambers, darkness best becoming their deeds of darkness. It is here that in the Scripture you have a command to take heed not only whom you hear for the preacher, and how you hear for its manner, but also what you hear for its matter. So, Mark says, "Take heed what you hear," (Mark 4:24). The physician may be authorized to practice, and yet prescribe dangerous medicine. The minister may be true to his office, and yet a false teacher as to his doctrine, and so he should be rejected. We must not only look to the messenger, but to the message. "And if any man (*whatever he is*) preach any other Gospel than this," (Galatians 1:8), "let him be accursed." These erroneous and seducing doctrines are the devil's tares, and preaching them is the devil's seed time. And if we would not have these tares to grow in our field, we must not be present where the devil sows them. For, we must know that a Christian may be poisoned to death, as well as starved. Therefore, it is the duty of Christians to take heed what they hear, unless they swallow down poison instead of wholesome food, soul-damning opinions instead of the sincere milk of God's word. "As new born babes desire the sincere milk of the word," (1 Peter 2:2), not the fantastical notions and opinions of vain minded men. Will you look to the food of your bodies, and will you not mind the food of your souls? Will you be careful that the bread you eat is indeed food for the body? And will you be so careless as to feed on the husks and poison of evil doctrine for your souls? Therefore, take heed what you hear, and who you hear, for sin first enters in by the ear. The Apostle says, "Evil words corrupt good manners," (1 Cor. 15:33). So, this first caution, when you are bid to prove all things, you do not have a liberty given to you to hear all sorts of preachers.

Secondly, when the apostle says, "prove all things," he never intended that men should be unstable in Christianity, skeptics in religion, wandering stars which are never fixed in the truths of the Gospel. They are not to be like seekers (for so they may very well be called) who settle nowhere, but are always finding out new truths, with their new lights, which usually in the end prove to be nothing but old errors. The Colossians were called on to seek rooting and establishing themselves in the faith (Col. 2:7).

Thirdly, in proving all doctrines that you hear, be sure you do not bring the Scripture to your opinion but bring your opinion to the Scripture. The Scripture teaches nothing but truth, and commands nothing but goodness. Many force the Scriptures to speak that which was never intended by the Holy Spirit, that they may seem to countenance those erroneous opinions which are divulged. They set the Scriptures as it were on the torturing rack to make them confess that which they never intended. This is how it was with the heretics of old, and this also is their practice in our days. They deal with the Scripture as she did with the oracle of Delphus, to make it speak what he meant. But this is the caution that I would give, do not bring your sense to the Scripture, but labor to carry away the Holy Spirit's sense from the Scripture.

Fourthly, in proving the doctrines that you hear, do not lean too much to your own understanding. Do not think that you are infallible that you are not over confident of your own opinion in controversial matters; especially if contrary to the judgment of those who are eminent for gifts and grace. Ponder the Scripture thoroughly, and seek to God by prayer, before you resolve in matters that are ambiguous. Proverbs 4:26, "Ponder the path of thy feet."

Having dispatched the cautions, I shall give the reasons why men must try the doctrines that they hear.

First, because erroneous and corrupt teachers may carry a very near resemblance to them that preach the truth. I have read of two painters, Parrhasius and Zeuxis, who contended for a mastery in their art. The one painted grapes so exactly that the bird came to pick at them. The other painter came to draw it, supposing that it had been real. There is such an affinity between sound teachers and seducing teachers that it is no easy matter for a man to discern between them.

But all is not gold that glitters. A notable text for this you have where the Apostle says, ""For such are false apostles, deceitful workers, transforming themselves into the apostles of Christ. And no marvel; for Satan himself is transformed into an angel of light," (2 Cor. 11:13). False apostles may transform themselves in this way, to be like the apostles of Christ. Ministers of the devil, factors of hell, transform themselves to be like ministers of Jesus Christ. Therefore, there is good reason that you should try all doctrines that you hear, whether they are agreeable to the word of God or not.

Secondly, because the word of God foretells that there shall be as many (if not more) false teachers under the New Testament, then under the Old Testament, and more in the latter days, then in the former days of this world. This is plain from that text of Scripture, "But there were false prophets also among the people, even as there shall be false teachers among you, who privily shall bring in damnable heresies, even denying the Lord that bought them, and bring upon themselves swift destruction," (2 Peter 2:1). They were of old under the law, they shall be with you under the Gospel. Although the Pharisees are dead, who corrupted the law, yet the same Spirit still lives in men, and will do so to the end of the world. The Apostle gives this as a reason why we should try such doctrines that we hear, because in the times of the New Testament, many false teachers will appear. "Beloved, believe not every spirit, but try the spirits whether they are of God: because many false prophets are gone out into the world," (1 John 4:1). Do not believe every man that says he has the Spirit, and that the Spirit teaches him that doctrine which he preaches, but try whether it is agreeable to the word of God or not. And the reason he gives is because there are many (not few) false prophets, and they have not gone into a corner, or bound up only one part of the world. Indeed, in former times, their nest was enclosed in one part of the world, in Germany, and especially Amsterdam. But now they have gone out into the whole world. Therefore, try the spirits whether they are true and of God. Try them before you trust them, and before you believe.

Thirdly, try all doctrines that you hear preached because false doctrines and heresies come from their publishers very craftily and slyly into the minds of men. There is not more agility showed by a cunning juggler than by these false teachers. They are subtle and cunning to pervert the minds of men. As the Apostle shows, "That we henceforth be no more children, tossed to and fro, and carried about with every wind of doctrine, by the sleight of men, and cunning craftiness, whereby they lie in wait to deceive," (Eph. 4:14). The word in the Greek has a great amount of emphasis here, ἐν τῇ κυβείᾳ which means *cogging of a die*. It is a word borrowed from cheating gamers that can throw with a die what they want to have come up. These teachers can as easily convey errors into the minds of men, as a cunning gamester can cheat with a die. We have had many such sly and subtle conveyances or else the truths of God could never have been perverted among us as they are. It is observable in Revelation 9:8 that the "locusts that came out of the East, had their faces like the faces of women." Interpreters expound them to be Jesuits, and factors for Rome. They had women's faces, which were insinuating and alluring countenances, inveigling, enticing and bewitching men with their follies. Of such the Apostle speaks, "For they that are such serve not our Lord Jesus Christ, but their own belly; and by good words and fair speeches deceive the hearts of the simple," (Rom. 16:18). Even as a foul faced whore paints her face with makeup to do their damnable errors with eloquent insinuations. Sometimes these false teachers tickle itching ears with such eloquent notions as many make them admired. And sometimes they suggest high privileges, unspeakable advantages by what they deliver. The devil did this to our first parents, "ye shall be like unto God's." Error must have good words to varnish over, and fair speeches, plausible, eloquent, and acute deliveries. By good words they deceive the hearts of the simple. And 2 Peter 2:1 the apostle sets forth their slyness in bringing "damnable heresies." Had Peter lived in our age, he would have been accounted a biter man, to call them heresies, yes, and damnable heresies. But they were privily brought in, and he says, "many shall follow their pernicious ways, and through covetousness shall they with feigned words make merchandise of you." With feigned words, this must be done, under the specious presence of truth and new light. They will mix some gold with copper, some truths with falsehoods. They will sweeten their baits, that they may take it sooner. For if the error was nakedly brought in, there is scarcely a man that would embrace it. It would appear in such an ugly shape, and so, they clothe it with a semblance of truth and piety.

Fourthly, you should try all doctrines that you hear before you believe them, because through the credulity that is in us, men of the most solid judgments are apt to be led away with novelties and deceived with error. We are by nature like the sand in the sea, moved with every wave, like reeds shaken with every puff of wind. A notable text for this is, "But I fear, lest by any means, as the serpent beguiled Eve through his subtilty, so your minds should be corrupted from the simplicity that is in Christ," (2 Cor. 11:3). The devil would not make use of a drunken or foolish creature, but a subtle serpent to beguile Eve in making her eat of the forbidden fruit. Now, the Apostle says I am afraid lest the devil by his subtle temptation should pervert your mind from the truth of the Gospel. This shows that there was an aptness in their nature to be turned aside to error. And moreover, even the most holy, the most understanding person in the mysteries of God are but in part enlightened. We see through a glass darkly (1 Cor. 13:12). And though they would not willingly mind you, yet through the remainder of ignorance and corruption that is in them, it is possible that they may take error for truth. Therefore, no man's piety or learning should so far blind us as to believe whatsoever he speaks, without bringing it to the touchstone of the word. For we must not build our faith on human authority, but divine authority. We must imitate the noble Bereans and search the Scriptures daily whether those doctrines that we hear are the truth of God and the word. They were commended for this in Acts 17:11. O! beloved, take nothing on trust, on the authority of the preacher, and weigh all things in the balance of the sanctuary. You must do this with the doctrines you hear, as you do with gold. A man will not take gold without weighing it. O! there is much falsehood in opinion as there are in metals, so, weigh all things. It is not what this man says, regardless if he is Peter or Apollos. It does not matter if he is eminent in learning and religion. But what God says in the Scripture is what counts, for the Scriptures are the rule of faith. Whatever is not according to this rule, reject it. It is the dross of man's corrupt brains, and do not receive it as the gold of God's pure word.

Now, it may be said, you have given various reasons why we should not believe doctrines we hear before we have tried them. But what rules or directions can you give so that such weak ignorant Christians as I am should be able to try and judge of such doctrine that I hear from the preacher? I will endeavor both in general, and in particular, to give an answer to this great question. And I hope it will be of great use to us in these erring times when false teachers and false doctrines so much abound.

First, take this general rule. Be sure you make the word of God to be the standard by which you try and prove all doctrines that you hear. And if there is anything preached (although it should be preached by an angel from heaven) that is not according to the word of God, do not believe it. This is the prophet's direction, "To the law and to the testimony: if they speak not according to this word, it is because there is no light in them," (Isa. 8:20). By *the law and testimony* we are to understand the word of God, which is his testimony. If anyone speaks otherwise then according to God's word, it is a clear and evident truth in them. I give you this direction because there are multitudes of vain people in these days who wave the written word of God and run to inspirations and revelations to try doctrines by. And these are not certain rules to go by. And so, by this means they entertain satanic delusions, and not heavenly inspirations. But I would desire such seriously to mind this one text of Scripture. It is, "And this voice which came from heaven we heard, when we were with him in the holy mount. We have also a more sure word of prophecy; whereunto ye do well that ye take heed, as unto a light that shineth in a dark place, until the day dawn, and the day star arise in your hearts," (2 Peter 1:18-19). The written word of God is more sure in regards to us than if we should hear a voice from heaven. And that is the reason why Dives in Luke 16 desired that some extraordinary course might be taken to prevent his brethren from coming to hell. So, he desired Lazarus might be sent from the grave to forewarn them, and he thought they would believe. Abraham sent him to Moses and the prophets instead, "If they will not hear them, neither would they be persuaded though one should rise from the dead." If we should hear a voice in the air, we must not believe that voice, but we must believe what we find on record in the word of God. "The secret things belong unto the LORD our God: but those things which are revealed belong unto us and to our children for ever, that we may do all the words of this law," (Deut. 29:29). This I mention to show you that men that pretend so much to rely on revelations and leave the written word of God, are in a way ready to run into Satanic delusions and gross mistakes.

    A second general direction about trying such doctrines as you hear is this, *viz.*, clear principles of truth must rather be maintained then disputed. It is a rule in philosophy that principles against principles are not to be disputed. And this rule holds good in divinity as well. We must not dispute such principles as these, *viz.*, whether Christ is the Son of God, or the Scripture is the word of God, or the resurrection of the body, or the salvation of saints, or the damnation of sinners, or the judgments to come, or eternal life. Such fundamental principles as these are to be maintained, but not disputed.

    Thirdly, maintain no opinion stiffly until you have tried it thoroughly. Such is the instability of men's minds in this erroneous age, that one sermon many times shall pervert them more from the truths of the Gospel than twenty sermons will settle them back down again.

But it will be further said, such ministers and preachers as are both learned and godly differ in many things. One asserts this to be the truth, and another asserts that to be the truth, so, how shall a poor creature as I am judge whether such doctrines are truth or not?

For an answer to this, as I have in general directed you, so I shall now more particularly give you some rules and directions by which you are to try all doctrines that you hear.

First, whatever the word of God expressly holds forth to be believed, received, or whatever necessarily flows from Scripture by a natural and genuine consequence, though it is not found in Scripture in opened and expressed words this doctrine is sound and to be embraced. Whatever agrees with the genuine sense of any one place of Scripture, although it may seem not to agree with the literal sense of another place of Scripture, this doctrine is sound and to be embraced. Or whatever doctrine is agreeable to the end, intent and scope of Scripture, such a doctrine is sound and to be embraced.

But on the contrary, that doctrine which is not found in Scripture, which is not set on the foundation of Scripture, which cannot be drawn by a necessity or consequence from Scripture, if it is built on the tradition and inventions of men which add to the word of God, or detracts from the word of God, which wrests and perverts it, is to be abhorred. Whatever doctrine will not abide in the trial of the word, and will not abide in the light, that doctrine is false, and to be abhorred.

Secondly, whatever doctrine advances the grace of God in Christ, and debases man, that puts the crown of glory on God's free grace, that doctrine is sound.

But on the contrary, that doctrine which debases the grace of God in Christ, and advances the corrupt will of man, and which sets freewill against free grace, that doctrine is unsound.

Thirdly, whatever doctrine advances the will of God, as well as the grace of God, which shows what God would have us to do, as well as what he has promised to do for us, that doctrine is a true doctrine.

But on the contrary, that doctrine which agrees with free grace, but in the meantime gives liberty to men to live as they wish, which makes the will of God for obedience and the grace of God for salvation to be contrary to one another, that doctrine is a false doctrine.

Fourthly, that doctrine which advances all the attributes of God, the justice of God as well as the mercy of God, the holiness of God as well as the grace of God, and approves of and commends all those ways and paths which God has set out in Scripture for us to walk in, which teaches us faith and repentance, piety towards God, and charity towards man, that doctrine is sound and good.

But on the contrary, whatever doctrine robs God of his glory in any of his attributes, that makes God either unmerciful or unjust, *etc.*, or that sleights any one of those ways that God has laid out in Scripture for us to walk in is false and corrupt. Anything that disjoins the two tables of God, separating piety from charity, acts of righteousness from acts of holiness is corrupt. Let it pretend to be filled with so much charity and piety to

God, if it does not direct one to charity and righteousness to men, that doctrine is false and corrupt.

Fifthly, whatever doctrine discovers the sinfulness of vain thoughts, lustful imaginations, as well as sinful practices, that doctrine is true. But the doctrine which requires only outward reformation, and does not reach to purify the heart, that doctrine is unsound.

Sixthly, that doctrine which advances all truth, the directing of truth, as well as the comforting truth, the commanding truth as well as the promising truth, that advances both law and Gospel, that doctrine is sound.

But on the contrary, that doctrine which is pleasing to the corrupt nature of man, easy to flesh and blood, that makes way for looseness and profaneness, that doctrine is unsound.

Seventhly, whatsoever doctrine necessarily tends to settle and compose a crooked conscience by teaching us to have a foundation only on the merits of Christ for salvation, and not on our own good works, that doctrine is sound.

But doctrine which leaves a distressed, perplexed conscience without any sound foundation to rest on, by teaching men to place the stress of their salvation on the mutable will of man, this is not only uncomfortable, but and unsound doctrine.

Eighthly, that doctrine that tends to the advancement of godliness in a man's Christian course, which (as the Apostle speaks in Titus 1:1) "acknowledgeth the truth which is after godliness," which conduces to perfect holiness, that puts us onto diligent care to work out our salvation with fear and trembling, that helps on the work of grace in the soul, that tends to inform the judgment, reform the heart, and conform the life to the whole will of God, that doctrine is true and good.

But on the contrary, that doctrine which tends to allow licentiousness and libertinism, causing men to neglect the ordinances of God, and to grow weary of congregational worship, family worship, closet worship, that turns the grace of God into wantonness is a false doctrine. The doctrine that magnifies the death of Christ but destroys the life of Christ, that sets up the blood of Christ, the priestly office of Christ, but does not regard the commands of Christ, the kingly office of Christ, is a false doctrine. The doctrine that makes men confident in mercy but careless in repentance, that makes Christ merciful, but leaves them sinful, or at best, brings them to a form of godliness without the power of it, is a false, erroneous and dangerous doctrine. Truth always advances godliness, but erroneous doctrine is contrary to it. "But shun profane and vain babblings: for they will increase unto more ungodliness," (2 Tim. 2:16). We find in our day the fruit of vain babbling and disputes to be the broaching of such damnable opinions as these, *viz.*, that a man must not mourn for sin, must not confess sin, must not pray for pardon of sin. And so, three parts to prayer are taken away. So, concerning the decree of God, that if they are decreed to be saved, they shall be saved so let them live as they wish. And if they are decreed to be damned, so they shall be damned not matter what they do. Whereas, the doctrine of election and reprobation should be a spur to stir us up in pursuit after holiness. So, concerning the Law of God that it is no use to believers. And many such pernicious errors and doctrines are occasioned with a great amount of disputing. All of this tends to prove them to be false, for truth ever advances practical godliness in a man's Christian course.

Lastly, a doctrine of truth will be true when they are tried, for truth fears no trial; it is error that fears the light that creeps into houses and does not dare to appear in public. It sets itself on silly women, laden with corruption as the Apostle speaks in 2 Tim. 3:6, but does not dare counter with a knowing Christian. And therefore, it is that the Turks forbid any man to dispute against the Koran. And it is that, that the church of Rome will not allow the common people to read the Bible, but they must pin their faith on other men's sleeves and believe as the church believes. And some, they cause their errors and idolatries to be swallowed down. Where, if they were brought into the light, the weakness and sinfulness of this would appear.

The sum of all this is this: when you hear any doctrine delivered, compare it with the word of God. If you find that is crosses any part of the Old Testament or New Testament, do not believe it. It is not the truth, but error.

These rules and directions for trying such doctrines as you hear may be of great advantage to you in these loose and erroneous times, if the Lord gives you hearts to make a right improvement of these things.

No, conscience does not tell me to convey anything I delivered to you, that is repugnant to the Scripture. But trust nothing that I preach until you have tried it. And if you find anything disagreeable to the written word, reject it. *Prove all things. Hold fast to that which is good.*

SERMON 3:
A Christian's Great Enquiry

"And brought them out, and said, Sirs, what must I do to be saved? And they said, Believe on the Lord Jesus Christ, and thou shalt be saved, and thy house," (Acts 16:30-31).

This text is propounded by way of interrogation. The manner of its composure intimates that it is the confusion of a perplexed mind, the question of a distempered and distressed soul. It is a question from a soul that is about the business of the greatest moment in the world. There are many critical, curious and controversial questions that men enquire after in these days. But this question on that poor jailor here asked, is a question of the greatest concern that ever can be made by any man. It was no less than this: what he might do to be saved?

The question seems to be the expression of a man in great anguish, and great consternation of mind, and truly the matter the question is about is such as might trouble the whole world. As a solemn divine answered one that came to him saying, "Sir, I am troubled about my salvation." He replied, "Friend, that is a business that might trouble the whole world." So here this poor man cries out to Paul and Silas, "What must I do to be saved?"

I shall not spend time about the explanation, but shall dispatch what I have to say in a practical prosecution of these words. Before I come to the points of doctrine, I intend to handle various circumstances and observations about the text. There are three concurrent circumstances about the words, from where three observations will arise.

1. From the consideration of the condition of man that propounds this serious question. The man was a jailor, a calling in those times especially filled with infamy because the followers of Christ were most of all in chains and jail when oppressors and men of violence escaped free. Yet, see here, that the jailor is an object of pardoning mercy. Here observe the following.

That men of the most despicable condition in the world may become the objects of God's pardoning mercy. Salvation is not impaled within the rank of the rich and honorable of the world, but sometimes men of the lowest rank become the objects of God's mercy. Pardoning grace reaches sometimes to the vilest and most notorious sinners in the world. Mark 2:17 says that Christ came "not to call the righteous, but sinners to repentance."

2. From the consideration of the occasion or manner of this jailor's conversion, for it is said, "In the night there was a great earthquake in the prison." The keeper was awakened out of his sleep, and when he arose, he saw all the prison doors open. In thinking that all the prisoners had been gone, he was in a great perplexity in his mind, fearing what would become of him. Now, God made this a means to cause this man to look after salvation, so that although he thought the escape of the prisoners might occasion the loss of his life, yet his care now was, what he might do to save his soul. He said, "Sirs, what must I do to be saved." In this observe the following.

1. That God by his providence many times brings it about that affliction shall be a means to make men look after salvation. Had not this poor man thought that he had lost his prisoners, God knows whether he had not lost his soul, or even whether he would have inquired about salvation. I have read of a Scottish divine who, being in great sickness, blessed God for it, for he says, this sickness of my body has been a means to save my soul. It is usual with God to make afflictions, of one kind or another instrumental to make men inquire after salvation.

2. The next thing to be considered is the great alteration that this providence made in the jailor. The poor man before was troubled to think that his prison doors were opened and it is said in verse 27, "That he drew his sword, and would have killed himself." But now we find no more talk of killing himself. But all his care was how to save his soul. Here observe the following.

That when once men come to make a diligent enquiry after heaven, there will then appear a great alteration in their passions and affections. This man's fear and care was not now how to get his prisoners back again. But his care now was what he should do that he might no longer be a prisoner to Satan. Not how to keep other men in bonds, but what he should do to free himself from the devil's bonds. O! the wonderful change that conversion works in the soul! It not only changes the conversation, but the very passions and affections are changed.

These observations are only transient, and not directly intended in the text.

Now I shall come to handle both the inquiry that the jailor makes, and the resolve that the apostle gives.

First, the jailor's inquiry is, "Sirs, what must I do to be saved?"

This question, or perplexed query, arises from a two-fold spring, or from two kinds of passions or affections in man.

1. It arises from fear. The man came in trembling and said, "Sirs, what shall I do?" Inquiries, when they are vehement, have mixtures of fear with them. As if he should have said, "I may lose my life, and my soul too, O but sirs, tell me how I may save my soul, and then it is no matter what happens with my life." There was a mixture of fear in this question, *what must I do* by reason of the evil I have done.

2. It flowed from the affection of hope. There would have never been an inquiry made if there had not been some hopes of mercy. The question, "what must I do?" argues some measure of hope. After impossibilities we often make no inquiry. We make no inquiry how we may climb up to heaven. We make no inquiry about how we can fly like a bird in the air. Why? Because these things are not possible to be done by men. But the things that are attainable are the objects of our inquiry. Now, what must I do to be saved? This argues that there was some hope in this man's heart of doing something.

The text contains in it these two particulars. 1) What must I do to be saved? 2) A full and satisfactory answer to the inquiry, "Believe on the Lord Jesus Christ and thou shalt be saved."

Now before I give you the point of doctrine, from the jailor's question, observe these six particulars about the manner and form of the expression.

1. He does not say, what evil shall I do? He that had done so much evil already would not add more sin to it. He would not add sin to sin, but he says, what good shall I do?

2. He does not say, what good words shall I speak? Or What good profession shall I make? But, he asks what good shall I do? It is not good words, it is not a good profession which will bring a man to heaven. Many cried *Lord, Lord,* that never entered into the Kingdom of Heaven.

3. It is not said, what may I do? as if it were indifferent whether he might do it or not. But he saw there was a necessity of doing something, *what must I do?*

4. It is not said, what must another man do? But he *asks what must I do?* As I cannot live by the food that another man eats, as I cannot go to heaven by the grace which another man does.

5. It is not said, what must I *know*, but what *must I do?* There are many times high flown speculations are found in men's minds, when there are no gracious dispositions in their hearts. But it is not knowing, but doing that will bring a man to heaven. John 13:17, "If ye know these things, happy are ye if ye do them." The devils know more than all the sons of men. They know much good even though they do much evil.

6. It is not said, what must I do to get my prisoners again? But he asks, what must I do to get to heaven, to save my soul? And this indeed is the inquiry,

about all inquiries. In this way you have some advertisements from the form of expression used here by the jailor.

The DOCTRINE is this: that above all things in the world, this is the most needful thing for the sons of men to make an inquiry into, namely, what must they do to be saved?

In handling this proposition, I shall first premise some cautions, secondly, give you some reason, and then thirdly, apply it all.

The cautions are three. First, though it is the most needful thing in the world for the sons of men to inquire after, *viz.*, what must I do to be saved, yet take this caution to heart. That though we must inquire what we must do, yet we must not expect to be saved by *doing*. A full expression to this purpose is found in Job 7:20, "I have sinned, what shall I do unto thee, O thou Preserver of men?" The interrogation implies an absolute negation, what shall I do? That is, "I can do nothing to satisfy your justice, to pacify your wrath, or procure your love and favor. Lord I have grievously sinned against you and if you look for reparation and satisfaction at my hands, I am in no way able to make that." Job speaks like a poor forlorn, broken debtor, to his rich and incensed Creditor. God is arresting him for his debt, which he is in no way able to satisfy. Therefore, he throws himself at his feet, and cries out, "Sir, I confess, I owe you much, but I have nothing to pay, and I am not able to make you the least amount of satisfaction for what I owe you. So it is this way with all mankind since the fall of Adam. God entrusted us with a great stock, but we have lost it all, and have become bankrupt, deeply indebted. We owe a thousand times ten thousand talents of gold to God. And we are not able to make the least satisfaction to his divine majesty, for all the wrong and dishonor we have done to him by our sins. We may indeed do something to God as a payment of our duty, but we can do nothing as a payment of our debt which we owe to him. Therefore, though there must be an inquiry made, asking what must I do to be saved? Yet, remember this, that no man is saved for *doing*.

2. Though no man is saved for doing, yet an inquiry must be made, *what must I do?* Because, no man can be saved without doing. According to that great Saint Augustine, "Though God made you without yourself, yet he will not save you without yourself." Indeed, my doing is not the cause of God's saving me but is a cause without which God will not save me. God saves no man for his doing, yet God will not save any man without his doing. God is not so prodigal of heaven as to throw it into those men's laps that will take no pains for it. Heaven is a goal, and unless you run you shall never obtain it. Heaven is a crown of life, but unless you are faithful to death, you shall never wear it.

3. A third caution is this, that inquiry after salvation does not exclude lawful inquiry and care after things of the world. God never intended that heaven should so monopolize and impale your care and inquiry so that you should look after nothing but heaven. You may have heaven and still be in the world too. You do not need to do as Socrates did, who because of his worldly estate hindered him from studying philosophy, that he threw it all into the sea and said, "I will destroy you, lest you should destroy me." You do not need to cast

away your estate. You may make inquiry after the things of the world and heaven too. Always provided, that your first and chief care is after heaven, and heavenly things, and your worldly care is subordinate to that.

These are the cautions that you should heed. Now consider some reasons.

First, we should, above all things, make an inquiry what we must do to be saved, because the soul is the most excellent thing in the world. It is clothed with Scripture with this special designation, "the precious soul." The body is but a shell, the soul is the pearl. The body is the case, the soul is the jewel. Therefore, make it your great work how to save your soul, because it carries a greater excellency with it, then all the world besides. Julius Cesar was accustomed to say of Cicero, that he was negligent in things belonging to himself, but diligent in things concerning the commonwealth. So, should we be negligent in things concerning our bodies in comparison of things concerning our souls.

Secondly, the inquiry after the soul's safety is the ready way to procure the welfare of the body. There is no man who is wise for his own person that is not wise for his soul. Matthew 6:33, "But seek ye first the kingdom of God, and his righteousness, and all these things shall be added unto you." Make it your great bargain to buy heaven, and God will place things in the world over and above what you seek spiritually, as riches and honor were given to Solomon, 1 Kings 3:12. Indeed, God will not always give the particular temporal blessing that you crave, or think you stand in need of, for he knows what we want better than we ourselves. But though he does not always hear us according to our will, yet he always hears us according to our needs. For the Apostle says in 1 timothy 4:8, "Godliness hath the promise of the life that now is, and of that which is to come." Of blessings of this life conditionally, so far as they conduce to our good, but of the life to come, absolutely. It is a notable passage we read in Exodus 1:21, "And it came to pass, because of the Midwives feared God, that he made them houses." The midwives feared God and God took care of them. If you take care of your soul, God will take care of your body.

Thirdly, make an inquiry to save your soul, because there is so much inquiry made by the devil to destroy your soul. 1 Peter 5:8, "Be sober, be vigilant; because your adversary the devil, as a roaring lion, walketh about, seeking whom he may devour." In the original language it says, "whom he may drink up at one draft." Satan envies our restored condition, that we should enjoy that paradise of bliss which he once had, and out of which he was cast down. And so, it is that he has become our irreconcilable enemy and is continually tempting and disturbing us of his infinite hatred of God and goodness. As the leopard bears such a natural hatred against men, that if he sees a picture of a man, he will tear it to pieces. So, the devil, if he sees the image of God in us, by all means he seeks to destroy us. Chrysostom says, "If the devil watches, will you sleep?" If the devil goes about, will you sit still? If the devil makes and inquiry what souls he might devour and damn, why then should not the sons of men make it their work to inquire how to save their souls?

Reason 4. Make this inquiry, because if you lose your soul, you have the greatest loss that is imaginable, for there is not a loss beyond it. To lose the soul is to bid farewell to God forever, farewell to Christ, farewell to a kingdom, and farewell to all society with saints and angels forever and ever. O! that word *ever* is the greatest aggravation of this loss. It is not a loss to be repaired. Lose your soul and you have lost all. It is a lasting loss, a loss that is irrecoverable. It is a good observation that Chrysostom has, "Nature has so ordered the parts of the body that a man has two eyes, two hands, two feet and two ears. So that if a man loses one eye, he can see with the other, or lose one leg and he can go on with the other, or lose one ear and he can hear with the other. But God has given you one soul, and if you lose that, you lose everything." O! consider that, and make this inquiry, "What must I do to save my soul?"

Use 1. I now come to make some useful application. If it is so, that above all things in the world you should make this your great inquiry, what must I do to be saved? Then, this is a rebuke to those that make assiduous inquiry about matters of a lesser moment, but never make inquiry about matters of salvation. There are a multitude of men in this age that puzzle themselves and trouble their minds with notions and critical questions, but never put this question to their souls, "Lord, what must I do to be saved?" O! how justly blameworthy are they that study curious and nice questions about Christianity, which serve only to obscure the clear truth of the Gospel. And in the meantime, they do not mind this great and necessary question, "What must I do to go to heaven?" Truly, we live in an age full of critical questions, in which all the dogmatic points of religion are called into question. But if God does not prevent it, these trivial questions will jostle out this necessary question, "What must I do to be saved?" Of all the questions, there are two question most necessary for a person to ask, and most comfortable for a minister to resolve them in. The one is "What shall I do to be saved?" and the other is "How shall I know that I shall obtain salvation?" Of all questions these are the greatest. And as Christ said (speaking of love to God and love to our neighbor), "This is the first, and greatest commandment, and the next is like to this." So I say, this is the first and greatest question, what shall I do to be saved? And the next question is likened to this: How shall I know I will be saved? The first is our foundation of happiness, and the second, of all our comfort.

2. It is for rebuke to those that make inquiry after the body, and things pertaining to its welfare, but never make inquiry after salvation. There are many men in the world, who (in the language of those sensual men of Psalm 4:6) cry out, "Lord who will shew us any good?" But they never make inquiry how they themselves may become good. These men are like him that came to the physician's inquiry, how he might cure the disease on his finger, but never asked how he might cure the consumption in his lungs. Many men make inquiry after trivial things of the world, but they do not inquire how they may get an interest in Jesus Christ, how they may escape hell, and get to heaven. Now what folly and madness is it for a man to be solicitously careful for those things which he shall have without this care, and to be negligent and careless about those things which he has

no promise to obtain without assiduous carefulness! He is not careful to obtain grace and glory, for they are not to be expected without seeking, and diligent seeking at that (Matthew 6:33). But outward things shall often cast off one from seeking heavenly things.

3. It is for rebuke to those that make inquiry how to damn themselves, but do not inquire how to save themselves. The drunkard inquires where wine and strong beer is to be had. The adulterer (as Solomon says) inquires where the house of the harlot is. In this way many men inquire how they may undo their souls. But, O how few are there that cry out with this poor jailor, "Sirs, what must I do to be saved?"

Use 2. The next use shall be by way of trial, to put you on a search whether you have put this question to its conclusion, whether you have resolved this question in your souls, that God indeed has brought you into an estate of salvation. Now that you may know this, consider these three particulars.

First, has God taken those methods with your souls that he takes with those who he intends to save? But you will say, what are those methods that God takes with a sinner whom he intends to save? I answer, first, God enlightens that man's mind so, as that he makes him see his sins to be exceedingly sinful, and himself to be exceedingly miserable. You have an admirable text for this in Job 33:27-30, "He looketh upon men, and if any say, I have sinned, and perverted that which was right, and it profited me not; He will deliver his soul from going into the pit, and his life shall see the light. Lo, all these things worketh God oftentimes with man, To bring back his soul from the pit, to be enlightened with the light of the living." It is God's usual way in bringing a sinner to hell, to represent his sins to him in the eyeglasses of the law, to cause him to see them to be exceedingly sinful, to cause him to confess his sinfulness, how he has perverted the way that is right. Paul said he was alive without the Law, but when the Law came, then he saw his sin to be exceedingly sinful. "Was then that which is good made death unto me? God forbid. But sin, that it might appear sin, working death in me by that which is good; that sin by the commandment might become exceeding sinful," (Rom. 7:13). Sin in its own nature is so exceedingly evil that it cannot have a worse name given to it than its own, sinful sin. Beloved, if the Lord has dealt in this way with you, so as to make you see your sins to be exceedingly sinful, and yourselves to be exceedingly miserable, know, this is the method that he takes with that soul which he intends to bring to heaven.

A second method that God takes with a sinner to save his soul is this, God puts him into a condition of spiritual astonishment, to see himself as an undone creature, altogether unable to save himself. And he does not know who will undertake that work for him. This is plain in the text, "Sirs, what must I do to be saved?" It is a question filled with astonishment and a mind that is very perplexed. When God once casts a man out of self-sufficiency, self-righteousness and self-ability, this is a good step towards heaven.

A third method that God takes with a sinner is this, God presents Jesus Christ to his soul, as the most desirable object in all the world. He sees sin to be exceedingly sinful, himself to be exceedingly miserable, and then he sees Jesus Christ to be exceedingly desirable. You whose souls can bear you witness that God has taken these very methods with you, know for your comfort, that these are the very methods that God takes with that soul whom he intends to save.

Secondly, you may discern whether God has brought you into an estate of salvation by those impressions which Jesus Christ will work on the hearers of those whom he intends to save. Now there are four impressions in this.

First, God causes the authority and majesty of the word, at some time or another, to fall on the conscience of that man with great conviction whom he intends to save. "For the preaching of the cross is to them that perish foolishness; but unto us which are saved it is the power of God," (1 Cor. 1:18). The power of God in his word shall be felt on the conscience of that man whom God brings into a saving estate. Therefore the Apostle expressly says, "For this cause also thank we God without ceasing, because, when ye received the word of God which ye heard of us, ye received it not as the word of men, but as it is in truth, the word of God, which effectually worketh also in you that believe," (1 Thess. 2:13). The word of God has an effectual work, and a majestic authority, on those that will be saved. It is mighty in operation in those that believe, transforming them into the very image of itself. It works what it prescribes, it enables the soul to come up to every duty, no matter how hard it is to flesh and blood, to hate every sin no matter how pleasant that sin might be, or profitable. It is active and operative as the Apostle says in Hebrews 4:12, "sharper than any two-edged sword," it effectually binds the conscience, rectifies judgment, subdues the will, and the sinner cannot stand out against it.

The second impression that God makes on the heart of that man that shall be saved, is this, he is brought into an obedient frame to obey the commands of God. The Law of God is not burdensome but pleasing, and delightful to him. He has a universal respect to all God's commands. David says, "Therefore I love thy commandments above gold; yea, above fine gold," (Psa. 119:127). And the Apostle says, "And being made perfect, he became the author of eternal salvation unto all them that obey him," (Heb. 5:9).

Thirdly, if God brings you into a saving condition, he makes this impression on your heart, that you have become as industrious to have your nature sanctified as your soul to be saved. "For we ourselves also were sometimes foolish, disobedient, deceived, serving divers lusts and pleasures, living in malice and envy, hateful, and hating one another," (Titus 3:3).

The last impression is this, if God saves your soul he will bring you into a believing state and cause you to lay hold on Christ by faith. And this leads me to the second point, which is the resolve that the Apostle gives this poor man crying out, *viz.*, "Believe on the Lord Jesus Christ, and thou shalt be saved."

At first blush one would think that the Apostle's resolve should not quiet at all the heart of this distempered man. Paul and Silas bid the man to believe. Might not he have replied, "I can as well make a world, I can as well work miracles, and overturn mountains, as believe by my own power, therefore, why do you bid me to believe?"

To this I answer, though it is true, that every command of God is difficult to the flesh. A man can as well make a world as make a good prayer. A man as well can subdue an army of men, as subdue one lust. Yet know for your comfort, that this is the tenure of the Gospel, that when the Lord calls for anything at the hand of his elect children, he does with that command convey a power into their souls to enable them to fulfill that command. If God bids a man to believe, the work will be done soon. In Ezekiel 36, the Lord commands to make a new heart, then to make a new world. Therefore, in the same place he promises to "give a new heart." And in another place, in Colossians 3:5, it is said, "mortify your lusts." Now a man cannot do this of himself, but the same God that bids you to kill your lusts will kill them for you. "Who is a God like unto thee, that pardoneth iniquity, and passeth by the transgression of the remnant of his heritage? he retaineth not his anger for ever, because he delighteth in mercy. 19 He will turn again, he will have compassion upon us; he will subdue our iniquities; and thou wilt cast all their sins into the depths of the sea," (Mic. 7:18). Again, God bids you to repent, but you are no more able to repent or to shed one tear for sin then a rock is to give out water. But God will give you a repenting heart. He has promised to give repentance and remission of sin. I implore you to observe this, that commands in Scripture do not show what the creature can do, or what he should do by his own natural power. But such commands in Scripture are charged on the creature to let him know what God will do for his elect. If we put forth sanctifying abilities that God gives us, God will add assisting grace to enable us to do what of ourselves we cannot do. Therefore, we should pray with St. Augustine, *Lord give what you command, and then command what you please.*

In the next place, observe the difference that is between the solve that Paul and Silas give to this question, and the resolve that Peter gives to the same question. "Then Peter said unto them, Repent, and be baptized every one of you in the name of Jesus Christ for the remission of sins, and ye shall receive the gift of the Holy Ghost," (Acts 2:38). Paul and Silas gave this answer, "Believe and be saved." There is much of God's mind in this, that different answers are given by the Holy Ghost to one and the same question. Both their answers are true. Peter says, "Repent and be saved," to show that faith which is not joined with repentance is but a presumptuous confidence. Paul says "Believe and be saved," to let you know that repentance which is not joined with faith is only a legal sorrow. Therefore, one says believe, the other says repent, to show that you must join both together. Had only this answer been given, "Believe and be saved," men would have said, that is a short cut to heaven. It is just believing. Peter says, "Repent and be saved," to show that both must come into the Christian's practice, that faith and repentance must go hand in hand together, if you expect to be saved. Now, I note this because there are some men that are all for believing on Jesus Christ, and not at all for repentance and mourning for sin. These make Peter's answer to be no answer at all. Then there are others that are all for repentance, they are troubled in spirit, and distressed in their mind. They wish their heads were water and their eyes a fountain of tears. They think by their sorrow for sin to make an atonement to God. But they do not at all rest on Jesus Christ by faith. Now, these men make Paul's answer to be no answer at all. But remember, you must repent and be saved with Peter, and you must believe and be saved with Paul.

But I shall briefly only speak to the answer which Paul and Silas here gave. And from this observe this doctrine, that it is the duty of all those that expect salvation to believe in Jesus Christ.

But I think I hear some say, if all this is true, surely, then, salvation may be had on very easy terms. For, do not all believe on Jesus Christ? God forbid that any should be so wicked as not to believe on their savior. I answer, indeed there are many that have a kind of belief, an historical belief, a national belief, even a common dead faith like Simon Magnus had, even as the stony ground had and as the devils have who tremble. This kind of faith a man may have and still go to hell.

But there are few in the world who have a lively precious genuine faith which the Scripture indeed accounts believing in Christ and which, whosoever has shall never perish but have everlasting life. There are few that are willing to receive Christ as he is tendered in the Gospel, to receive Christ as king to rule them as well as a Jesus to save them. There are few that are willing to receive a naked Christ, Christ with his cross as well as Christ with his crown. There are few that are as ready to give themselves to Christ for sanctification as to take Christ for justification. Most people love the priestly office of Christ, to purchase salvation for them, but they do not live the kingly office of Christ, to conquer corruption in them. They would be willing to have Christ receive them into heaven, but they are not willing to receive Christ into their hearts. In the day of their calamity when they lie on their sickbeds, and the terrors of death take them over, then, none but Christ can save them, none but Christ. But in the day of their prosperity, when the world smiles on them, and riches and health surrounds them, then Christ is not esteemed by them and they see no beauty in him that they should desire him. For there is no wicked man in the world that will take Christ on Gospel terms in the time of his health and outward prosperity. And moreover, most people think that it is the easiest matter in the world to believe, but it is believing, they think, that is in their power to believe at any time, whenever they want, and that they can believe in time enough even to the point they lie on their death beds. They are not considering that God puts for the same almighty power when he works faith in the soul, as he did when he raised Jesus Christ up from the dead, as the Apostle shows. "And what is the exceeding greatness of his power to us-ward who believe, according to the working of his mighty power, 20 Which he wrought in Christ, when he raised him from the dead, and set him at his own right hand in the heavenly places," (Eph. 1:19). It is as impossible for a man, by his own power, to make himself believe, as to create a world or give being to himself. And consider here, that every assent to the word is not believing. Bellarmine says that believing is only a bare assent to the word, but if saving faith only consisted in a bare assent to Scriptural truth, then there would be multitudes of believers in the world. But God does not own such believers.

2. Consider that faith is not a presumptuous confidence. The nature of faith does not consist in this. It is a grace of God worked and fashioned in the heart of a humble sinner who discerns his sins to be enough to damn him, and all his own righteousness useless to be too little to save him. Therefore, he gives himself over and rests and relies wholly on the righteousness of Jesus Christ, expecting salvation only by him.

Now, should we take a survey of all the sons of men, where should we find them that do in this way believe on Jesus Christ? How few are there in the world that feel their sins pressing sorely on them, that see all their righteousness and religious performance to be things of no value in the point of justification? How few that find in their souls longing desires after Jesus Christ, that they may be found in Christ, not having their own righteousness? That soul rests itself, rests its burdens, on Jesus Christ, resolving that if they perish, there they perish in him? Certainly beloved, should men try their hearts by this description of faith, there would be found but few believers in the world.

Now, for a word of application. And first, from the inquiry that the poor man makes, "Sirs, what must I do to be saved?"

Learn from this to take heed that you do not make an inquiry after toys and trifles, and in the meantime neglect the great matters of eternal life. It was a sordid spirit in that king Sardanpalus who would be spinning and carding among the women, when he should have been ruling and governing his kingdom.

There are many men that are of this base and ignoble temper. They spend their time, strength and labor in base and sordid employments, and in the meantime neglect the great and important affairs of a heavenly kingdom.

A second inference is this, if there are so few in the world that make an inquiry how to be saved, then here we must conclude that there are but few in the world that shall be saved. There are many in the world that never came so far as with that moral young man spoken of in Matthew 19. He asked, "What good things shall I do that I may inherit eternal life?" Yet, people will not ask as the jailer did, "What must I do to be saved?" O! beloved, if most of the world never make an inquiry after heaven, then how few in the world shall come to heaven?

Secondly, from the resolve that the Apostle gives to the jailor's question, "Believe on the Lord Jesus Christ," rest on Christ for your salvation, on his mercies, on his blood, and on his righteousness. Learn here what a great benefit and privilege the children of men have by living under a covenant of grace, for although they cannot be saved by what they can do themselves, yet they may be saved by what Jesus Christ has done for them. You cannot be saved by all your doing, but you may be saved by believing, by resting and relying on Jesus Christ, expecting salvation by what he has done and suffered in your stead, on your behalf. Had we lain under a Covenant of Works, then it would be "Do this and live." But a Covenant of Grace says, "Believe and live." The condition of the Covenant of Works is that we should give an exact and perfect righteousness of our own to God, the righteousness of another will not serve the turn. And in this covenant, little will not be accepted for much, the will for the deed. The sentence of absolution shall be pronounced if you are found without spot or blemish, completely righteous. But the sentence of condemnation will come on you if you are found unrighteous in the least point. This covenant does not speak one word of hope or help, mercy or peace, to a poor lost sinner, but pronounces him accursed for the least transgression, for the least deviation from the righteousness of the Law of God. And there is no place left for repentance, no place left for mercy, on the breach of this covenant. Adam, by one sin, made all his prosperity miserable, and the Apostle says, "For as many as are of the works of the law are under the curse: for it is written, Cursed is every one that continueth not in all things which are written in the book of the law to do them," (Gal. 3:10). So that there is no possibility of life by the Covenant of Works because in our lapsed state, in our state of corruption, the Covenant of Works is impossible to be fulfilled by us. Since the day that sin came into the world, that Adam ate the forbidden fruit, not one man ever fulfilled the Covenant of Works, for, "there is no man that sinneth not," (1 Kings 8:46). And, "If they sin against thee, (for there is no man which sinneth not,) and thou be angry with them, and deliver them over before their enemies, and they carry them away captives unto a land far off or near," (2 Chron. 6:36). And Ecclesiastes 7:20 says, "In many things we offend all." And, "For in many things we offend all. If any man offend not in word, the same is a perfect man, and able also to bridle the whole body," (James 3:2). O! then, what cause do we have to admire the infinite and unspeakable mercy and goodness of God in making this Covenant of Grace with man a sinner. This is the New Covenant when the former was violated, which is as it were a plank after a shipwreck. That when a man had voluntarily transgressed the righteous Law of God, and by this, justly deprived both himself and his posterity of that life and blessedness which was promised in that covenant and fell under the death and curse which God had threatened for breaking and transferring of that covenant. Yet, notwithstanding that such should be the infinite mercy of God, that he should not insist on the forfeiture, that he should bind us up in the Covenant of Works but takes us out of the hands of his justice and puts us into the hands of his mercy. He does not deal with us according to our defects, but according to the richness of his grace, in his unsearchable wisdom (when men and angles were at a loss). In him we find out that there is a remedy to help and relieve a poor forlorn lost sinner that is cast down by the Covenant of Works, not sparing his only begotten son, Jesus Christ the Righteous, the Mediator of the New Covenant (Heb. 12:24). Jesus satisfied God's justice, slain that enmity which was between God and us, and made peace for us. For, in this Covenant of Grace, the righteousness of Christ and satisfaction made by Christ, is held forth and tendered to the justice of God. The Surety is punished and the debtor is spared. "All we like sheep have gone astray; we have turned every one to his own way; and the LORD hath laid on him the iniquity of us all," (Isa. 53:6). Because, "He is despised and rejected of men; a man of sorrows, and acquainted with grief: and we hid as it were our faces from him; he was despised, and we esteemed him not," (Isa. 53:3). John says, "My little children, these things write I unto you, that ye sin not. And if any man sin, we have an advocate with the Father, Jesus Christ the righteous: 2 And he is the propitiation for our sins: and not for ours only, but also for the sins of the whole world," (1 John 2:1-2). So, here mercy may be found to help and relieve a poor sinner, which is lost in the Covenant of Works. In the Covenant of Grace God accepts the will for the deed. He does not stand strictly on it for the sinner, as to cast the sinner out of favor for every transgression. But, "Like as a father pitieth his children, so the LORD pitieth them that fear him," (Psa. 103:13). God pities those that are faithful with him in covenant, those that strive to do the will of the Lord and fly to his grace for pardon and acceptance. Those that repent of their transgressions and promise and perform upright obedience. For, in this covenant there is a place for repentance and mercy for the penitent sinner. "Repent ye therefore, and be converted, that your sins may be blotted out, when the times of refreshing shall come from the presence of the Lord," (Acts 3:19). And, "He that covereth his sins shall not prosper: but whoso confesseth and forsaketh them shall have mercy," (Prov. 28:13). But under a Covenant of Works there is no place left for repentance nor mercy for the penitent. Here then we see the inestimable, the unspeakable benefit we have by a Covenant of Grace. For now, by laying hold on Jesus Christ, by a true and lively faith, by resting and relying on what he has done and suffered in our stead, and in our behalf, we may lay a rightful and infallible claim to the

Kingdom of heaven. "Believe on the Lord Jesus Christ and thou shalt be saved."

SERMON 4:
A Description of True Blessedness

"But he said, Yea rather, blessed are they that hear the word of God, and keep it," (Luke 11:28).

In the humanity of Jesus Christ such a luster and beauty shined and broke forth that even in such a despicable person as he was deemed to be, yet the very words which he spoke and the works that he did declared him to be no less than the Son of God; as in John 7:46 his very enemies confessed that never a man spoke as Christ spoke. He spoke better than any man spoke. By the words he delivered it was evident he was more than a man, but the works which he did spoke plainly with an audible voice concerning his divinity. And concerning the miracles which he wrought, it was said of many of them that "never was it thus done since the beginning of the world;" his miracles wrought admiration even in the hearts of those men in whom they wrought envy and malice against him. The miracle specified in this chapter, the dispossessing of a dumb man of the devil; this did spread abroad the fame and renown of Christ through many parts of the world, and though his enemies were so obstinate, that they would not (notwithstanding these miracles that he wrought) acknowledge his divinity, yet there was a young woman that slipped out of all the company and went to Christ and lifted up her voice saluting him in these words, saying, "Blessed is the womb that bore thee, and the paps that gave thee suck;"

though the Pharisees would not call him blessed, yet this young woman cried out, "Blessed is the womb that bore thee." And had this commendation been given to another, it might have made him proud, but it works a contrary effect on Christ; he rather gives her a rebuke than any thanks and tells her that "rather blessed are they that hear the Word of God and keep it." And so, I have brought you to the words of my text. But before I come to give you the doctrine which the words will afford, give me leave to speak something concerning the words of the woman's saluting Christ after this manner; the words which she spoke were a common proverb among the Jews. When any man had done something commendable—that was excellent and extraordinary—they would presently cry out to him, "Blessed is the womb that bore thee, and the paps that gave thee suck," from which I would note to you this much: that *good children are a great blessing and commendation to their parents.*

And here it is that you read so often in Scripture what a great blessing it is for a father to be the father of a good son, and a mother to be the mother of a good child (Prov. 10:1 and 15:20). And on the contrary, what a great curse it is for parents to bring forth wicked children into the world, "a wicked child is a shame to his father, and a heaviness to his mother" that brought him into the world.

The *use* I would have you make of this doctrine is this: you that have good children, that are instruments of the praise and glory of God, bless his name for them; and you that have bad children look on it as a stroke of God's heavy hand on you. Yet, this is only a point by the way, from the woman's speaking this way of Christ, "Blessed is the womb that bore thee, and the paps that gave the suck;" but Christ told her, "rather blessed are they that hear the Word of God and keep it." Christ says, "rather blessed," he does not say that his mother that bore him was not blessed, for she did bear him in her heart as well as in her womb. But Christ speaks this with a gentle loving rebuke to the woman that gave him this commendation; Christ says, "thou cryest out, 'blessed is the womb that bore thee,' but I say, rather blessed are they that hear the Word of God and keep it," so that from here note, from Christ's example, that *you must take a great deal of heed that you are not tickled with pride, whenever you hear yourselves or yours commended,* you see here Christ would give no way to their commendations of his mother.

And then again, "yea, rather blessed;" Christ says that those are rather blessed that hear the Word of God and keep it, than his mother that brought him into the world; from where we observe that *a believer that hears and obeys Christ is rather blessed in so doing, than the Virgin Mary was merely in bringing Jesus Christ into the World, though it were the happiest birth that ever woman brought forth.*

And O! how this should be a spur to hearers to make them obey and practice what they hear!

But I shall keep you no longer in the entrance into the words, and therefore I shall only give you something to note from the manner of the expression that Christ here uses, and then draw out the doctrine the words will afford. In the form of speech that Christ here uses, observe, it is not said, "blessed are they that hear the Word of God;" there are many sorts of hearers that come short of blessing, "but blessed are they that hear the word of God and keep it." The Greek word here is φυλάσσοντες (*phoulassontes*), *keep it.*

There are four sorts of hearers spoken of in Matt. 13 and three of them are bad, and but one is good which hears the word correctly; because we know that all that hear the word do not obtain a blessing.

It is not said, "Blessed are they that hear," but, "Blessed are they that hear and *keep* what they do hear."

It is not said, "Blessed are they that believe," (*observe that*) though this is true, yet it is not said so, lest men should think that a bare and naked believing were enough to entitle them to blessedness. There are many men that pretend to faith and assurance, and yet live only in duties, above hearing, and praying, *etc.* and therefore Christ says not, "Blessed are they that believe," but, "they that hear the Word and keep it."

It is not said, "Blessed are they that keep the Word in a disjunction from hearing," but they that keep the Word in a conjunction *with* hearing; blessed are you who hear *and* keep. There are many men that pretend to be high flown in their practice, and to keep what Christ commands them, but yet it is a disjunctive obedience, they will not hear; those are only blessed in Christ's esteem, that keep and hear the Word of God.

It is not said here in the text, "Blessed shall they be that hear and keep the Word of God," but, "Blessed are they that hear and keep the Word;" you shall not only be a blessed man when you come to heaven, but you are a blessed man while you are here on earth; you have "thy fruit unto holiness, and the end everlasting life," (Rom. 6:22).

Observe further, it is not said, "Blessed are they that hear and keep it," but, "Blessed are they that hear the Word of God and keep it." For you may hear errors and blasphemies and keep them and be accursed for doing so; but "blessed are they that hear the Word of God and keep it." And this should teach men to take heed, how they hear, and what they hear, and whom they hear, and that they hear nothing but that which is the Word of God. We read of some that follow teachers that "bring in damnable heresies;" (2 Pet. 2:1) (αἱρέσεις ἀπωλείας) "many shall follow (ἐξακολουθήσουσιν) their pernicious ways." Now such as these are not blessed, that hear men that bring in errors and heresies, but they are rather cursed.

Observe further, Christ does not say, "Rather blessed are they that hear my sayings and keep them;" but, "that hear God's Word:" for had Christ said, "Rather blessed are they that hear my Word," the people might have been ready to think that Christ entailed blessedness only to his own preaching, and to them that heard Christ personally teach here on earth. But says he, "Blessed are they that hear the Word of God," whether it is by Paul, or Apollos, or Timothy, or Titus, or any minister of Christ to the world's end. "Whoever shall hear the Word of God contained in the Scriptures, preached out of their mouths, and shall keep and obey it, they are rather blessed than my mother that bore me is, for that reason only of bringing me into the world." There is in this expression a secret glory put on the ministers of the Word, and this is the reason of that saying in Scripture, "He that believes shall do greater works than Christ did;" that is, a faithful minister should convert more souls that ever Christ did. It is true, Christ might (if he had so pleased) have converted every man that heard him, but he would not, lest men should thereby have undervalued his ministers, and have thought that none should convert souls but Christ; and therefore there were more converted by Peter and other apostles than there were by Christ himself, because he might hereby encourage men to the hearing of ordinary ministers.

There are some in the Church of Corinth (1 Cor. 1:12) that some of them said, "We are for Paul;" others, "We are for Apollos;" others "We are for Cephas;" and others, "We are for Christ." Now the apostle blames them that any of them should say, I am of Christ; there were some among them that said, "I do not care for hearing of Paul, or Apollos, or Cephas, I will hear Jesus Christ;" it was vanity in them to undervalue the ministry of Paul and Apollos, and to cry up Christ; it is a sinful crying up of Christ to cry down Paul and Apollos. And so, in these times for men to cry up Christ, and yet to cry down the ministry, is as sinful now as it was in the apostle's time; and therefore, Christ himself was careful to preserve the honor of the ministry that was to succeed him to the end of the world, "Blessed are they that hear the Word of God and keep it."

It is not said, "Rather blessed are they for hearing, and for keeping the Word," but, "Blessed are they that hear and that keep it." Blessed doers never come in with a "for," but only with an "if" or a "that;" the Lord does not bless you for your hearing, though you *should hear* as many sermons as there are days, but he blesses them that hear, and that practice what they hear. Hearing the Word and practicing and obeying it, are the qualifications or characteristic notes of such persons as shall be blessed by Christ; but not the *causes* of their blessedness.

And so, I have given you these seven notes from the form of speech Christ here uses. I shall now explain the words a little more to you, "Blessed are they that hear the Word of God and keep it."

What is meant here by keeping the Word you hear? You must know there is a double keeping of the Word, one in your memory, the other in your practice.

1. In your memories, this you have mentioned in Luke 2:19. It is said there that "Mary kept all these things, and pondered them in her heart," (συμβάλλουσα ἐν τῇ καρδίᾳ αὐτῆς). Our memories should be like the Ark of the Covenant in which the pot of manna was kept; the Word of God should be treasured up in or memories as the pot of manna was in the Ark. But this is not the type of keeping here spoken of, for there are many men that keep the Word in their memories, and yet never practice it in their lives.

2. There is a keeping of the Word in your practice. When you have a care which is a concern to sway your practice answerable to what you hear and know, and this is the keeping that is meant here, "Blessed are they that hear the Word of God and keep it;" that is, keep it in their practice, and make conscience to do what they hear and know.

The words being opened, their observation will be this: *that they are rather blessed that hear the Word of God and practice what they hear, than the mother of Jesus Christ was for bringing him into the world.*

Beloved, it is a point that I confess, had it not been in the Bible, it had been incredible that those that hear the Word and keep it should be rather blessed than she that bore Christ in her womb. That Christ should put a rather blessed on you, O man or woman that hears the Word of God and keeps it, than on the Virgin Mary for bearing Christ into the World; what a great privilege is this!

Beloved, it is worth noting what a different dialect is used between this woman here in the text and Elizabeth that was related to the Virgin Mary; this woman in the text cries out, "Blessed is the womb that bore thee, and the paps that gave thee suck." But Elizabeth, she says, "Blessed is she that believes," if the Virgin Mary had not borne Christ in her heart as well as in her womb, she would not have been a blessed woman.

Before I give you the reasons of this point, I shall only draw this inference from it, to confute the nonsense of the Church of Rome that venerates too much to the Virgin Mary; where they have one service for the glory of Christ, they have twenty for the glory of the Virgin Mary. They would make the world believe that she was without sin, and if so, why should Christ pronounce others rather blessed than she? This then is a confutation of the Church of Rome, that holds that the Virgin Mary had no original sin; and if so, then she should have been rather blessed than anyone else in the world. If that is true, then this text must needs be false, for Christ says here that "rather blessed are they that hear the Word of God and keep it" than she.

This confutes them because they venerate the righteousness and holiness and dignity of the Virgin Mary, that they undervalue the righteousness of Jesus Christ her son; they so *dote* on the Virgin Mary that they make her the great mediator for us to the Father. Where we say, and maintain, that Christ is the only mediator, for, "there is but one mediator between God and man, the man Christ Jesus."

Ministers had never more need to confute Popish doctrines and opinions than now. For never was Popery more likely to increase and flourish in this land than it is now, and therefore I give these glances concerning them because there is a great deal of danger, lest people are infected with these Popish fooleries. I speak like this on my own experience; I have been a preacher these 10 years, and in all that time I never perceived so many inclining towards Popery as I have done within these two months; since these late strange actions that have been done among us. I have seen many to stagger about our religion and have been strongly tempted to embrace and fall to Popery, which is the reason that induced me to make this digression.

We come now to the reasons of the point.

1. Because Christ counts such in near relation to himself, no, in nearer relation to him than his own natural friends, as in Mark 3:33-35. When they told Christ that his mother and his brethren were without seeking for him, he says, "Who is my mother or my brethren? Whosoever shall hear the Word of God and keep it, the same is my brother, my sister, and mother."

2. Because if you hear the Word of God and keep what you hear, you shall persevere and have the end of

your faith; in Matt. 7:24, Christ says there, "Whosoever heareth these sayings of mine and doth them, I will liken him unto a wise man which built his house upon a rock, and the rain descended and the floods came, and the winds blew, and beat upon that house, and it fell not, for it was founded upon a rock." So those only that hear the Word of God and practice it, shall have the end of their faith, and have their souls built on that rock Christ Jesus, that shall never be removed.

3. You are blessed in practicing what you hear, because thereby you may bring many others to blessedness. In 1 Pet. 3:1, the apostle says there, "Wives be in subjection to your own husband, that if any obey not the word, they may without the word be won by the conversation of their wives."

And those men that have been won to Christ by your good example, when they have come to appear before God in judgment, by seeing you they shall glorify God in the day of their visitation and shall bless God that by your means they were brought to heaven.

4. They that practice what they hear are blessed because, though they may not bring others to heaven, yet they are sure to come to heaven themselves; in Rev. 14:12-13, "Here is the patience of the saints, and here are they that keep the commandments of God and the faith of Jesus. Blessed are the dead that die in the Lord, they rest from their labour, and their works follow them;" those that keep the commandments of God and the faith of Jesus, they shall come to heaven though they bring nobody else there. Where a gospel life goes before, an angel's life shall follow after. You that lead gospel lives here, assure yourselves that you shall lead angels' lives

hereafter, and therefore makes conscience do and practice what you hear and know.

We come now to the application, and the use I shall make of it shall be threefold, for lamentation, consolation, and exhortation.

1. For lamentation, is it so that they are rather blessed that hear and practice what they hear in the Word than the Virgin Mary? O, then how should this consideration provoke you to lamentation, that when you may have the blessing on such terms as these, "Hear my Word and make conscience to practice it, and you shall be blessed," yet you reject your own mercy. O you perverse and hard-hearted man or woman, that will not practice what you hear; you reject your own mercy. The devil could not damn you if you would not damn yourself. You, O man, that let the Word say what it will, you will do what you want, but do you stand in the way of your own blessedness, and reject your own mercy?

And to set home this particular point on your hearts, give me leave to press it with these three or four considerations:

1. Consider that you who do not make conscience to practice what you hear, you provoke the Lord to take away the Word from you, that you shall not hear it at all. In Amos 8:9, because Israel was weary of the Word of God, and of his Sabbaths, saying "When will the new moon be gone, that we may sell corn, and the Sabbath, that we may set forth wheat?" Therefore, God says, "I will cause the sun to go down at noon, and I will darken the earth in the clear day, and I will send a famine in the land, not a famine of bread, or a thirst for water, but of hearing the Words of the Lord." God may take away the

Word from you, for your not profiting under it. In Matt. 21:43: "The Kingdom of God shall be taken from you and given to a nation bringing forth the fruits thereof."

2. Consider that your hearing, if you do not practice what you hear, will aggravate your damnation another way; in John 15:22, Christ says, "If I had not come and spoken unto them, they had not sin, but now they have no cloak for their sin." So, in Luke 12: 47, "That servant that knew his Lord's will, and prepared not himself, neither did according to his will, shall be beaten with many stripes."

It is an observation that one has on the prophecy of Isaiah from the 13th to the 24th chapter of that prophecy, you shall read there of many dismal denunciations of judgment, "the burden of Babylon," "the burden of Tyre," "the burden of Damascus," and of Moab, and of Egypt, and the "burden of the sea." The Lord commanded the prophet to pronounce a burdensome prophecy against many nations and people; but among them all there is "the burden of the valley of vision" in the 22nd chapter, and it is observed that this is the most burdensome of them all. The reason is because that was a place of vision and knowledge, where the Word of God was dispensed, and because of their sinfulness and unprofitableness, their burden is heavier than all the rest, because it is the burden of the valley of vision. Though other men may go to hell that live in those parts of the world where the Word was never taught, and where they never heard the voice of the glad tidings of salvation sounding in their ears, yet those that live where the Gospel is preached, and know and yet do not walk answerably, shall go to hell with a heavier burden than the other shall do.

3. Another consideration is this: that you are void of the love of God; you do not love him, nor he you, if you do not make conscience to practice what you hear; in 1 John 2:5, "Whoso keepeth his word, in him verily is the love of God perfected, and he that says he loveth him and keepeth not his commandments is a liar, and the truth is not in him."

I shall now speak something by way of exhortation to provoke you all in the fear of God to make conscience to practice what you hear and know; and to this end consider that God does look on all your knowledge and profession to be worth nothing, unless you practice what you profess. God looks on all your hearing and praying, *etc.* as nothing unless your conversation is answerable to it; and is it not a pity that for want of practice you should lose the blessing of all your hearing, and make it of no worth or esteem in God's account, that though you have a great deal of notional knowledge, he looks on you as an ignorant sort, and you that have heard so many sermons, as if you have never heard one all thy lifetime? It is said of the sons of Eli that they "knew not the Lord." Why they? Surely, they did know him, but because they were sons of Belial, and unholy and profane in their lives, therefore God did not account their knowledge and gifts to be anything, because they did not practice what they knew. O! then beloved, shall God account your hearing as nothing, and your praying as nothing, because you do not make conscience to practice what you hear and know?

You can have no persuasion in your own soul of the love of God towards you unless you make conscience to practice what you hear; in John 14:15, Christ says, "If you love me keep my commandments;" and therefore often in Scripture these two are put together: loving of God and keeping his commandments.

But now by way of consolation, I think I hear a poor soul say, "Are they only blessed that hear the Word of God and keep what they hear? Who then shall be blessed, for who is able to keep what he hears? I many times hear a duty commanded, but I am not able to perform it, and such and such things required, but I am not able to keep them, and such and such graces pressed to obtain, but I am not able to get them."

For your comfort, know that you lived under a covenant of works, you could never be a blessed man, for you are not able to perform its conditions. For that requires you to keep and fulfill the whole law of God *perfectly* and *personally*. But now being under a covenant of grace, God accepts your keeping of the Law if it is done sincerely, though it is but imperfectly, and though it is not done in your own person, yet if it is done in the person of another, the Lord accepts it. God says to us under a covenant of grace, "Believe and live, if you make conscience to keep the Word, though you cannot keep it, yet I will pardon you and accept you; and though you cannot keep the Law in your own person, yet if my Son keeps it for you, I will accept *his obedience* as if it were done by you." And therefore, you must not lie down under despondency of your mind, because you are not under a covenant of works, but under a covenant of grace, in which Christ accepts of sincere obedience though it is not perfect.

Know for your comfort that if you have a full purpose of heart to keep that which you hear, it is looked on by God as if you kept it. In Heb. 11:17, it is said there that "by faith Abraham, when he was tried did offer up his son Isaac," because Abraham did in the resolution and purpose of his heart determine to obey God in offering up his son, therefore the Scripture looks on it as done, though it were only in purpose, not actually.

Why so, you that are the son of Abraham, and have the faith of Abraham, those holy duties which you desire to perform better, as to pray better, and to hear better, and practice and live better, then you do; in divine account this is looked on as if it were really done.

FINIS

ANNEXED:
The Saint's Rest,
or Their Happy Sleep in Death

As it was delivered in a sermon at Aldermanbury
London, August 24. 1651.
by Edmund Calamy B.D.

"And when he had said this, he fell asleep," (Acts 7:60).

These words contain in them the happy closure and upshot of Stephen's life, in which we have three particulars.
1. The person that fell asleep.
2. The speech that he made, when he fell asleep.
3. What he did when he had finished his speech.

First, we have the person that fell asleep, and that was Stephen. He was a man full of faith, and full of the Holy Spirit, as you may see in Acts 6:5. He was the first martyr that ever suffered for the cause of Christ after Christ's ascension into heaven. Here, I might gather this DOCTRINE, *viz.*, that the best of men are subject to violent and unnatural deaths. Stephen, that was full of the Holy Spirit, was stoned to death; and John the Baptist that was full of the Holy Spirit from the very womb, was beheaded. Peter was crucified, and so was Andrew. Isaiah was sawed asunder. Jeremiah was stoned, and Zacharias was slain between the temple and the altar. But I shall pass this.

The second part of the text, is the speech that Stephen made when he fell asleep, that is, when he had finished his prayer, he fell asleep. Here observe, that it is an excellent way to close up our lives with prayer. To die praying is a most Christian way of dying. They stoned Stephen calling on God. After this manner Christ also died; he prayed, "Father, into thy hands I commend my spirit, and having thus said, gave up the ghost," (Luke 23:46). He did this that it might be a pattern to all Christians.

Prayer is a necessary duty at all times, but especially when we are a dying; and that for these three reasons.

1. Because when we are to die, we have the most need of good help, for then the devil is most busy, and we are most weak.

2. Because when we are to die, we are to beg the greatest favor we have of God, that is, that he would receive us into his heavenly Kingdom. Now prayer is the chief means to obtain this mercy, for it is the gate of heaven, a key to let us into paradise. Therefore, we have great reason to die praying.

3. Because when a saint of God is dying, he is then to take his last farewell of prayer. In heaven there is no praying, but it is all thanksgiving; there is no need to pray in heaven, therefore, we do not pray there. Now, a saint of God, when he is leaving this world, when he is to die, should see that it is fit that he should die praying.

I implore you to remember this pattern in the text. Stephen died calling on the Lord. Let us die praying, as that Emperor said, so may I say, it behooves a Christian to die praying.

Question. But what was the substance of Stephen's prayer?

Answer. He prayed for himself, and he prayed for his persecutors.

1. He prayed for himself, "Lord Jesus receive my Spirit," (verse 59).

2. He prayed for his persecutors, "Lord lay not this sin to their charge," (verse 60).

I will not enter on this part of the text, for it would swallow up all my time. Therefore, I shall wave it, and come to the third part, which is, by God's assistance, that I purpose to speak to, *viz.*, what Stephen did when he had finished his prayer. When he had said this, he fell asleep, that is, he died.

Behold here the magnanimity, the piety, and the Christian courage of Stephen. The people were stoning him and gnashing their teeth on him; and the good man dies with as much quietness of mind, as if he had died in his bed. He fell asleep, while they were stoning him. While he died he prayed, and while he prayed he died.

But what made Stephen die in this way quietly? Read the 55th verse and you shall see its reason. "Being full of the Holy Spirit, he looked up steadfastly into heaven, and saw the glory of God, and Jesus standing at the right hand of God." Behold, he says, "I see the heavens opened, and the Son of man standing at the right hand of God." This made him die with such a sweet, quiet and calm temper. He saw Jesus Christ standing at the right hand of God, ready to receive his soul, and that made him die with such an extraordinary quietness of mind.

Death in Scripture, especially the death of God's children, is often compared to a sleep. It is said of David, "That he slept with his fathers," (1 Kings 2:10). And it is said in 1 Thess. 4:13, "I would not have you ignorant concerning them which are asleep," that is, concerning them which are dead. And 1 Cor. 11:30, "For this cause many are weakly and sick among you, and many sleep," that is, many die. This expression is a metaphorical expression and will afford us many rare and precious instructions about death. And therefore, (by the grace of God assisting me) I desire to spend the rest of the time in the opening of this metaphor.

DOCTRINE: the observation is this, *viz.*, that when a child of God dies, though his death is so unnatural and violent, yet it is nothing else but a falling asleep. The death of a child of God, though stoned to death, though burnt to ashes, though it is so violent and unnatural, is nothing else but a falling asleep. When he had said this, *he fell asleep.*

Somnus est mortis imago, sleep is the image of death. There are many notable resemblances between sleep and death; some of which I shall speak to at this time.

1. Sleep is common to all men; there is no man that can live without sleep. A man may live long without food, but no man can live long without sleep. So, it is true of death. Death is common to all, it is appointed for all men once to die. And therefore, David said, he was to go the way of all flesh, all men must sleep the sleep of death, or else be changed, which is a metaphorical death.

2. As sleep arises from the vapors that ascend from the stomach to the head, and tie the senses, and hinder their operations, so death came into the world by Adam eating the forbidden fruit, and by the poison vapor of sin, that brought death on him, and all his posterity.

"By one man sin entered into the world, and death by sin, and so death passed upon all men, for that all have sinned," (Rom. 5:12). Had Adam never sinned, Adam should never have died. But God said, "In that day thou eatest the forbidden fruit thou shalt die the death." Sin brings *omnimodam mortem*, all kinds of death; it brings temporal death, spiritual death and eternal death. Now, because all men are poisoned with the poison of sin, therefore, all men must sleep the sleep of death. It is sin that has poisoned all mankind.

3. As a man, when he goes to sleep puts off his clothes, and goes naked into bed, so it is with us when we come to die. We came naked into the world, and we must go naked out of the world. As we brought nothing with us into the world, so we must carry nothing with us out of the world. And therefore, death in Scripture is called nothing else but an unclothing of ourselves, (2 Cor. 5:4). Death to a child of God is nothing else but the putting off of his clothes. The body of man is the soul's clothing; and death is nothing else but the unclothing of the soul. It is just like a man going to bed and putting off his clothes. Peter calls it, "The putting off our earthly tabernacle," (2 Peter 1:14). Our bodies are the soul's tabernacle, and death is putting off this tabernacle.

Beloved, when we come to die, we shall be stripped naked of three *things:*

1. We shall be stripped naked of all our worldly honor, riches and greatness.

2. We shall be stripped naked of our bodies. *And,*

3. Which is above all, we shall be stripped naked of our sins. And that is the happiness of a child of God,

he shall put off, not only his mortal body, but the body of sin.

4. In the fourth place observe, as no man knows the time when he falls asleep, a man falls asleep before he is aware. So, no man can tell the specific time when he must die. There is nothing so certain as that we must die, nothing so uncertain as the time when we shall die. Death comes suddenly even as sleep comes on a man before he is aware.

5. Observe, as children and infants, because they do not know the benefit of sleep, are very upset to go to sleep. Many times, the mother is forced to whip the child to bed. Even so, it is this way with most of God's people, because they do not study the benefit of death. They do not know that death puts an end to all miseries and sins, and opens a door to let us into everlasting happiness, and that we shall never see God or Christ before we die. I say this because God's people do not study the benefit of death, therefore, they are like little children, loathe to die, loathe to go to bed. And therefore, death is called *the king of terrors* (Job 18:14). Death is terrible to many of God's children, because they are infants in grace, and because they do not know the benefit of death.

6. Observe, as when a man is fast asleep, he is free from cares, and free from troubles. Let it thunder (as it thundered not long since, as you know) yet a man that is fast asleep, while he is asleep he does not hear it. Let the house be on fire, while the man is asleep, he does not see it, neither is he troubled at it. So, it is like this with the death of God's children. When God's children sleep the sleep of death, they are free from the thunders of this world, they are free from all cares, from all troubles, they

go to their graves as to their beds, and rest in quietness, and are not sensible of any troubles that are in the world, For Abraham does not know us, (Isa. 63:16). So also see 2 Kings 22:20. "Thou shalt be gathered into thy grave in peace, and thine eyes shall not see all the evil which I will bring upon this place." When a child of God sleeps the sleep of death, he does not feel, nor is he sensible of any of the calamities or sad providences of God on the earth.

7. When a man goes to sleep, he goes to sleep for a certain time. In the morning he wakes up out of his sleep. So, it is this way with the sleep of death. And therefore, death is called *a sleep*, because we must all awake in the morning of the resurrection. We are in the grave, as in our beds, and when the trumpet of God, and the voice of the archangel shall sound, we shall all rise out of our grave, as out of our beds. Death is but a sleep for a certain time.[11]

8. Sleep is a great refreshing to those that are weary and sick, and when the sick man awakes, he is more lively and cheerful then he was before he fell asleep. And therefore, sleep is called *Medicus laborum, redintegratio virium, recreator corporum*, the great Physician of the sick body, the redintegration of man's spirits, the reviver of the weary body. And so it is with death, when God's people awake out of the sleep of death, they shall be more active for God, then ever they were before; when you lie down in the grave, you lie down with mortal bodies; It is sown a mortal body, it shall rise up an immortal body, it is sown in dishonor,

---

[11] Calamy is not teaching soul sleep. He is explaining the metaphor. Later, he will show that others teach the damnable doctrine of soul sleep.

but it shall rise up in honor, it is sown a natural body, but it shall rise up a spiritual body (1 Cor. 15:42-43).

9. As in the morning when we arise out of our beds, we then put on our clothes. So, in the morning of the resurrection, we shall put on a glorious body, like the glorious body of Jesus Christ. We shall put on *stolam immortalitatis*, the garment of immortality.

10. As no man when he lays down to sleep, knows the direct time when he shall awake, so no man can tell when the resurrection shall be. They do but comfort you, who say, that the general resurrection shall be such or such a year; for, as no man can know the minute when he shall awake out of his natural sleep, no more can any man know when we shall arise from the sleep of death.

11. As it is a very easy thing to awake a man out of sleep, it is but jogging him, and you will quickly wake him up. So, it is like this with the sleep of death, it is as easy for Jesus Christ to awake us out of the sleep of death, as it is for me, or you to awake a man out of sleep in bed.

12. As when a man arises in the morning, though he has slept many hours, no, suppose he could sleep twenty years together, yet notwithstanding. When he awakes, these twenty years will seem to be but as one hour to him. So, it will be at the Day of Judgement, all those that are in their graves, when they awake, it will be *tanquam somnus unius horae*, but as the sleep of one hour to them.

13. Lastly, and most especially, as sleep seizes only on the body, and the outward senses, but does not seize on the soul, the soul of man is many times most busy when the man is asleep. And God has here revealed

most glorious things to his children in dreams, when they have been asleep. God appeared to Abraham and many others in dreams; the body sleeps, but the soul awakes. So, it is like this with the sleep of death, the body dies, but the soul does not die. There are some men that are not afraid to teach you that the soul sleeps as well as the body, and that when the body dies and falls asleep, the soul likewise continues in a dull lethargy neither capable of joy nor sorrow, until the resurrection.

Beloved, this is a very uncomfortable, and a very false doctrine. They endeavor to prove it from my text. They say that Stephen, when he died, fell asleep. This is true in regards to his body, *he fell asleep*, but his soul did not fall asleep. Only that which was stoned fell asleep, which was only his body. For when he was being stoned, he saw Jesus Christ standing ready to receive his soul into heaven. The Lord Jesus said, "receive my spirit." Stephen's soul could not be stoned, though his body was stoned. So, when Jesus Christ was crucified, his soul was not crucified, I mean, when his body was killed, his soul was not killed. Indeed, he endured torments in his soul, which made him cry out, "My God, my God, why hast thou forsaken me?" But yet his soul did not die. So, when Stephen died, his soul went to Christ.

It is true, when a child of God dies, the soul goes to sleep. How is that? The soul goes to sleep in a Scriptural sense, that is, it goes to rest in Abraham's bosom (O blessed sleep!) it goes to rest in the embraces of God; it goes into the arms of its Redeemer, it goes to the heavenly Paradise, it goes to be always present with the Lord. But take heed of that wicked opinion, to say, that the soul sleeps in an Anabaptistical sense, that is, that it lies in a strange kind of lethargy, neither dead, nor alive, neither capable of joy nor sorrow, until the resurrection. Though Stephen's body fell asleep, yet his soul did not fall asleep, but immediately went to Jesus Christ in heaven. In this way, I have given the explanation of the words.

Now give me leave to make some application of all this to ourselves.

If the death of God's children is nothing else but a falling asleep, then let this comfort us against the deaths of our godly friends, though they die unnatural and violent deaths; though they are stoned to death, though they are burnt to ashes, though they are sawn in two, *etc.* Here is a message of rich consolation, which as a minister of Christ, I hold out to you this day, *viz.*, that the death of a child of God, let it be after whatever manner it will, it is nothing else but a falling asleep, he goes to his grave, as to his bed. And therefore, our burying places are called *dormitoria*, our sleeping-house. A child of God, when he dies he lies down in peace, and enters into his rest. And, as a man, when he is asleep, is free from all the cares and troubles that he has in the day time. So, the people of God, when they are fallen asleep, they are free from all the miseries and calamities, crosses, losses and afflictions that we are troubled with. Therefore, give me leave to say to you, as Christ did to the women that followed him to the cross bewailing and lamenting him, "O daughters of Jerusalem, weep not for me, but weep for yourselves, and for your children," (Luke 23:27-28). So, I say, O do not weep for those that are dead in the Lord, that are fallen asleep in Jesus Christ They are at their rest; they do not know the troubles that we are troubled with at all. Abraham does not remember us. They are not sensible of our miseries and afflictions. Let us weep for ourselves, and for the miseries that are coming on us; and let us know, that when God's children die they do but lie in their beds until the morning of the resurrection, and then they shall put on the garment of immortality, and their bodies shall be made like the glorious body of Jesus Christ. And know one thing more, which is everything, *viz.*, that when the body of a child of God falls asleep, his soul immediately goes into the arms of Christ, and their lives forever in the embraces of Jesus Christ. Though the body falls asleep, yet the soul is received into Abraham's bosom. I entreat you, comfort one another with these words.

Use 2. Let me implore the people of God that they would look on death, not as it is presented to us in nature's mirror, but as it is set down in a Scriptural way. Nature presents death in a very terrible manner; and it is true, death is very terrible to a man outside of Christ. But, to you that are in Christ, the sting of death is taken away, death is nothing else but a quiet and placid sleep, putting off of our clothes, and a going to bed until we awake in the morning of the resurrection. Death to a child of God is nothing else but putting off his earthly tabernacle. It is going from an earthly prison into a heavenly palace, a hoisting up the sail for heaven. It is like letting the soul out of prison, as a bird out of the cage, that it may flee to heaven. It is a change from a temporary hell to an eternal heaven. It is going out of Egypt into Canaan, and therefore, called in 2 Peter 1:15, not the death of the man, but the death of his sins. It is the pilgrim's journey's end, the sea-man's haven; an absence from the body, and a presence with the Lord. Let all God's people look on death through Scriptural glasses, and consider it as it is, sweetly represented in this text! Remember blessed Stephen stoned to death, and yet falling asleep. And remember also that excellent saying of Augustine, that a child of God should be as willing to die as to put off his clothes, because death is nothing else to him but a sleep, and a departure from misery to everlasting happiness.

Use 3. To implore you all every night when you go to bed, to remember this text, and especially to remember these four things.

First, when you are putting off your clothes, remember that you must shortly put off your bodies.

Secondly, when you go into your beds, remember that it will not be long before you must go down into your graves.

Thirdly, when you close your eyes to sleep, remember that it will not be long before death will cause you to close your eyes.

Fourthly, when you awake in the morning, remember that at the resurrection you must all arise out of the grave, and that the just shall arise to everlasting happiness, but the wicked to everlasting misery.

It is a saying of a heathen man, that the whole life of a man should be nothing else but *meditatio mortis*, a meditation of death. And it is the saying of Moses in Deut. 32:29, "O that men were wise, that they understood this, that they would consider their latter end." Beloved, it is the greatest part of wisdom every day to remember our later end, that man is the only wise man, and happy man in life and death, that is ever mindful of his death.

But before I make an end, I must answer one *question, viz.*, Whether the death of the wicked is not in Scripture compared to a sleep, as well as the death of the godly?

Answer. I answer, that wicked men in Scripture are said to fall asleep when they die. It is said of idolatrous Jeroboam, that he slept with his fathers. Of Baasha and Omri, those wicked Kings, (1 Kings 16:6, 28), that they slept with their fathers.

Question. But then the *question* will be, in what respect is the death of the wicked compared to a sleep?

Answer. Even as a man which is asleep, sometimes has no benefit, rest or ease by it, when the sick man awakes, he is many times sicker than he was before he went to sleep. Some men are greatly disquieted in their sleeps by hideous and fearful dreams. Nebuchadnezzar, when he was asleep, had a most scaring dream, and when he awoke he was amazed there with. So, it is with a wicked man. Death to a wicked man is a sleep, but it is a terrifying sleep, it is that the soul goes immediately to hell, where it is burned with fire that never shall be quenched, and where the worm that never dies is always gnawing on it. The body that indeed lies in the grave asleep, but how? Even as a malefactor that sleeps in prison the night before he is executed, but when he awakes he is hurried and dragged to execution. So, the wicked man falls asleep in death, but when he awakes, he awakes to everlasting damnation. But now a child of God, when he sleeps the sleep of death, he sleeps in his Father's house, and when he awakes, he awakes to everlasting happiness.

Use 4. And this makes way for the fourth and last use, which is a *use* of very great consequence. And it is to implore you all, that you would labor to live, that when you fall asleep, you may sleep a happy sleep. There is the sleep that the wicked man sleeps when he dies, and there is the sleep that the godly man sleeps when he dies. Now I implore you, labor so to live, that when you fall asleep, your sleep may be a happy sleep to you, that when you awake in the morning of the resurrection, it may be an awakening to you.

Question. But then the great question will be, how shall I do this?

Answer. I shall give you four or five helps for this:

First, if you would sleep a happy sleep at death, then you must labor to sleep in Jesus Christ. It is said in 1 Cor. 15:18, "Then they also which are fallen asleep in Christ." And in 1 Thess. 4:14, "If we believe that Jesus died and rose again, even so them also which sleep in Jesus, will God bring with him." What is it to sleep in Jesus? To sleep in Jesus is to die in the faith of Jesus Christ.

2. To sleep in Jesus, is to die with an interest in Jesus Christ, to die as a member of Christ united to him, as our head. For, you must know that the dust of a saint is part of that man who is a member of Jesus Christ, and every believer when he sleeps in the dust, he sleeps in Jesus Christ, that is, he lies in the grave, and his dust is part of Christ considered as mystical. Christ, as a *head,* will raise it up, and cannot be complete without it. Now then, if you would ever sleep a happy sleep, labor to get

a real interest in Christ. Labor to live in Christ while you live. And then, when you fall asleep, you shall be sure to sleep in Jesus. There are many that would have Christ to receive their souls at death, and that say with dying Stephen, *Lord Jesus receive my spirit.* But if you ever would have Christ to receive your souls when you die, you must be sure to receive him into your souls while you live, if you would ever have him to receive you into heaven, you must receive him into your hearts. No man makes a will, but he says, *Imprimis,* I bequeath my soul to Jesus Christ my Redeemer. But how do you know that Jesus Christ will accept this legacy? If your soul does not have Christ's image on it, if it is not regenerated and renewed, Jesus Christ will never own it. You may bequeath it to Christ, but the devil will claim it if your soul has the devil's image on it. *If it is a swinish, polluted, unbelieving, unregenerate soul, you may bestow it on God, but the devil will recover it out of God's hands.* Pardon me using that expression, it is not mine, but Augustine's. Beloved, if you would ever reign with Christ when you die, he must reign in you while you live. And if you would ever sleep a happy sleep, you must live in Jesus that you may sleep in Jesus.

  Secondly, in the second place, if you would ever sleep a happy sleep at death, then you must take heed of overcharging yourselves with worldly cares. A man that is full of cares cannot sleep, therefore, when men would sleep, they lay (as the Proverb is) all their cares under their pillow. They labor to shut all cares out of their mind. O! take heed that you do not murder your souls by the cares of the world. Beloved, a man that eats out his heart with worldly cares, will never sleep a happy sleep, the cares of the world will choke all the good seed of the word of God. And therefore, as men, when they sleep, lay aside all worldly thoughts. So, if you would ever sleep a happy sleep, take heed of too much seeking and caring for the things of this world. Remember what you have heard this day, and that will regulate and moderate all your cares. Naked you came into the world, and naked you must go out of the world. Why should we take care for that which we do not know who shall enjoy it after us when we leave it to them when we die?

Thirdly, if you would ever sleep a happy sleep when you die, you must take heed of sucking too much of the pleasures of this life. A man that eats a full supper, will sleep very disquietly, therefore, they that would sleep quietly use to eat but light suppers. For, when a man's stomach is over-charged, it takes away his sweet sleep from him. So, if you would ever sleep a happy sleep when you come to die, O! take heed of sucking too much of the pleasures of this life. Take heed of eating too large a meal of worldly delights, and of creature comforts. These worldly pleasures will make the sleep of death unquiet unto you. O! do not let Dalilah's lap, deprive you of Abraham's bosom! Remember that David by Bathsheba's embraces lost the embraces of God, I mean, the sense of the embraces of God, their joy and comfort.

Fourthly, if you would ever sleep a happy sleep in death, then labor to work hard for heaven while you live. O how delightful is sleep to a weary man? When a man has taken pains all day, as the traveler that has traveled all day, or the ploughman that has been at work all day, how quietly, how soundly does he sleep in the night? O Beloved! If you would ever sleep a happy sleep at death, then labor to work out your salvation with fear and trembling, and give all diligence to make your calling and election sure. The more you labor for heaven the better, the sweeter will your sleep be when you come to die. And remember this, that as much sleeping in the day time, will hinder a man's sleep at night. So, you that idle away the time of your providing for heaven in your day, you that sleep away the minute on which eternity depends. O! you will have a sad sleep when death seizes on you. Take heed, therefore, of sleeping while you live, so that your sleep in the night of death may be comfortable to you.

Fifthly, lastly, if you would ever sleep a happy sleep when you die, then take heed of the sleep of sin. Sin in Scripture is compared to a sleep, "Awake thou that sleepest," that is, you that sin. Sin is such a sleep as brings the sleep of death. Sin brings the first death, and sin brings the second death. All miseries are the daughters of sin no matter what they are. If you would sleep a happy sleep, and have a happy awakening at the Resurrection, then take heed of the sleep of sin, "Awake thou that sleepest, arise from the dead, and Jesus Christ shall give thee life," (Eph. 5:14; see also Romans 13:11-13). With that I will conclude. I pray you mark it well, for it was a text that converted Saint Augustine, "Knowing the time, Beloved, that now it is high time to awake out of sleep, for now is our salvation nearer then when we believed. The night is far spent, the day is at hand, let us therefore cast off the works of darkness, and let us put on the armor of light; let us walk honestly as in the day, not in rioting and drunkenness not in chambering and wantonness, not in strife and envying, but put you on the Lord Jesus Christ, and make no provision for the flesh, to fulfill the lusts thereof."

FINIS.

Other Works by Christopher Love at Puritan Publications

The Christian's Combat Against the Devil (eBook, Print and Audio Book)

> Are you ready for battle? Is the devil just a figment of your imagination? In the evil day will you stand firm? Do you have on the whole armor of God? What is your strategy for spiritual warfare? More Info »

Heaven's Glory

> What will heaven be like? Love's work is a masterful treatment of Colossians 3:4 showing the glory and happiness prepared for the elect in Christ. This work parallels Love's book, "Hell's Terror". More Info »

Christ's Ascension and Second Coming from Heaven

> Are you ready for him to return from heaven? This wonderful work on eschatology by Christopher Love not only combats the impossibility of the 1000 year reign of Christ on the earth, but especially comforts believers in the immanent reality of Jesus' return from heaven. More Info »

A Christian's Directory

> Every Christian needs spiritual direction in the basics of the Christian Life. Christopher Love

masterfully applies 1 Cor. 7:30-31 and creates for us a "directory" to demonstrate how Christians should always walk, whether in joy, or in mourning, whether in prosperity, or in poverty. A very convicting read!

A Treatise on Hell's Terror

Jonathan Edwards said this was one of the best works he'd ever read on the doctrine of hell. I'd have to agree. After reading this work over the years, it is by far one of the top works on hell. Don't let this one pass you by. More Info »

The Hearer's Duty and Other Works

This rare set of works by Christopher Love covers hearing the sermon as God intended without distraction while you sit in church listening to the preacher. He also covers buying and selling goods as a Christian steward. It is one of his best works. More Info »

The Last Words and Letters of Christopher Love

Christopher Love's last words are eminently practical and highly spiritual. This work includes his last sermon ever preached on Job, and the non-before published "Vindication" of the charges that were laid against him before he was beheaded. More Info »

Also consider these new releases:

How to Hear the Preaching of God's Word with Profit by Stephen Egerton (1555–1621)

The Wickedness, Humiliation, Restoration and Reformation of Manasseh by C. Matthew McMahon

The Nature, Danger and Cure of Temptation by Richard Capel (1586–1656)

5 Marks of a Biblical Disciple by C. Matthew McMahon

5 Marks of a Biblical Church by C. Matthew McMahon

Seeing Christ Clearly by C. Matthew McMahon

The Christian's Desire to See God Face to Face by Richard Sibbes (1577–1635)

Gospel Worship, or, The Right Manner of Sanctifying the name of God in General, in Hearing the Word, Receiving the Lord's Supper, and Prayer by Jeremiah Burroughs (1599-1646)

www.ingramcontent.com/pod-product-compliance
Lightning Source LLC
LaVergne TN
LVHW041545070426
835507LV00011B/945